Cambridge Elements ≡

Elements in Epistemology
edited by
Stephen Hetherington
University of New South Wales, Sydney

T0328645

THE EPISTEMIC CONSEQUENCES OF PARADOX

Bryan Frances
United Arab Emirates University

CAMBRIDGE
UNIVERSITY PRESS

CAMBRIDGE
UNIVERSITY PRESS

University Printing House, Cambridge CB2 8BS, United Kingdom

One Liberty Plaza, 20th Floor, New York, NY 10006, USA

477 Williamstown Road, Port Melbourne, VIC 3207, Australia

314–321, 3rd Floor, Plot 3, Splendor Forum, Jasola District Centre,
New Delhi – 110025, India

103 Penang Road, #05–06/07, Visioncrest Commercial, Singapore 238467

Cambridge University Press is part of the University of Cambridge.

It furthers the University's mission by disseminating knowledge in the pursuit of education, learning, and research at the highest international levels of excellence.

www.cambridge.org
Information on this title: www.cambridge.org/9781009055963
DOI: 10.1017/9781009052948

© Bryan Frances 2022

First published 2022

A catalogue record for this publication is available from the British Library.

ISBN 978-1-009-05596-3 Paperback
ISSN 2398-0567 (online)
ISSN 2514-3832 (print)

Cambridge University Press has no responsibility for the persistence or accuracy of URLs for external or third-party internet websites referred to in this publication and does not guarantee that any content on such websites is, or will remain, accurate or appropriate.

The Epistemic Consequences of Paradox

Elements in Epistemology

DOI: 10.1017/9781009052948
First published online: June 2022

Bryan Frances
United Arab Emirates University

Author for correspondence: Bryan Frances, bryan.frances@yahoo.com

Abstract: By pooling together exhaustive analyses of certain philosophical paradoxes, we can prove a series of fascinating results regarding philosophical progress, agreement on substantive philosophical claims, knockdown arguments in philosophy, the wisdom of philosophical belief (quite rare, because the knockdown arguments show that we philosophers have been wildly wrong about language, logic, truth, or ordinary empirical matters), the epistemic status of metaphysics, and the power of philosophy to refute common sense. As examples, the author examines the Sorites paradox, the Liar paradox, and the Problem of the Many – although many other paradoxes can do the trick too.

Keywords: paradox, metaphysics, wisdom, philosophical progress, common sense

ISBNs: 9781009055963 (PB), 9781009052948 (OC)
ISSNs: 2398-0567 (online), 2514-3832 (print)

Contents

1 Introduction

Most philosophers agree that outside of the formal parts of philosophy, we cannot offer rigorous *knockdown proofs* of philosophically substantive theses. We might be able to prove things in formal logic, mathematics, and decision theory, and those results can be philosophically important. But knockdown proofs of philosophically substantive theses in regular, nonformal philosophy? Ha ha … nope. Most of us without hubris abandon the goal of giving knockdown (informal) proofs of philosophically substantive conclusions.

As a result, many of us retreat to offering reasonable, "interesting," yet hardly foolproof arguments for theses of the form "This solution to the problem is true/false." If one has struggled for a number of years with such projects, then one will, unless wildly confident in one's abilities, have moments of despair about even this more modest goal. After all, you will, if you are sufficiently reflective and honest with yourself, eventually see that there always are good (yet inconclusive) objections to your arguments that you cannot block. So, we often *retreat once again*, watering down our conclusions to "This view has such-and-such going for it" or "This criticism of such-and-such view is no good – unless, of course, the criticism gets changed radically in order to maneuver around the problems I've detailed here."

Another disappointment is that most philosophers now admit that philosophy, by itself, is not nearly as strong as science when it comes to showing how common sense is mistaken. In the olden days, philosophers advanced bold arguments purporting to prove that many of the average idiot's beliefs were laughably false, to put the point boldly and unkindly. Now we hang our heads and mumble that although science is up to the task, our profession is too weak to deliver the goods. Some of us even feel intellectually tough in admitting this loudly, without the mumbling. It's akin to standing up and saying, "Yes, I am a sinner! I am! I admit it!"

So, conventional wisdom says "No knockdown arguments in normal philosophy" and "No refutations of common sense from philosophy." What would be really crazy would be philosophical arguments that are *both* knockdown *and* refutations of common sense. That would refute both parts of conventional wisdom with one blow.

That's the way things seemed to me – until recently. Now I suspect, but certainly do not believe, that we can give knockdown proofs of highly counterintuitive theses, refuting both parts of conventional wisdom with one blow. However, we have to do it in a new way, starting from *exhaustive analyses of philosophical problems*. Bizarrely enough, we may be able to prove philosophically substantive theses without taking any stand on the solutions to any of those problems we are analyzing.

To get an idea how this might work, pretend that each of the following three claims regarding some intellectual problem is highly intuitive: C_1, C_2, $\sim (C_1 \ \& \ C_2)$. It's child's play to derive a contradiction from them. Your first reaction to such a situation is to conclude that at least one of the three claims is false. That may seem a safe inference to make. However, if you decide to be more cautious, to look for proofs instead of merely persuasive arguments, you will realize that such a conclusion is hasty. For one thing, maybe some contradictions are true. For another thing, maybe there is some subtle equivocation in the trio of claims that blocks the application of the derivation of the contradiction (so they don't really have the logical forms they appear to have). For yet a third thing, maybe elementary logic is flawed in some deep fashion, so the obvious derivation applies to the three claims but the inferences aren't truth-preserving.

Having such a cautious attitude doesn't preclude one from confidently drawing conclusions, however. We can be *extremely confident* in concluding that the truth lies in one of the following four possibilities:

- one or more of the three claims C_1, C_2, and $\sim (C_1 \ \& \ C_2)$ isn't true
- the trio of claims is true but there is some subtle equivocation or other linguistic difficulty present in them that makes the derivation of the contradiction not apply, so no contradiction results from the trio
- the trio is true and there is no such linguistic difficulty (so the derivation does apply just as we expected) but one of the elementary sentential inference rules in the derivation isn't truth-preserving, so no contradiction results
- the three claims are true, the derivation goes through as expected, the inference rules are truth-preserving, and thus a contradiction is true too.

If we realize that the claim "An equivocation or similar linguistic complication was present that ruined the obvious application of the derivation" is philosophically counterintuitive in the rough sense that its truth would require a huge change in our beliefs, then we can safely conclude that *whatever the truth is about the intellectual problem in question*, it's philosophically counterintuitive, since, as we just saw, there are exactly four options and each has that quality. Therefore, our analysis of the problem itself, without taking any stand on its solution, has yielded two interesting results: one, the disjunction of the four claims is true; two, a philosophical argument proves that there exists a philosophically counterintuitive truth (viz. one of the disjuncts, although we don't know which one). In this Element, I show that something akin to this scenario applies to many (not all) philosophical problems. As we will see, its consequences are philosophically significant.

I have long had the gut feeling that many philosophical paradoxes are amazing in the sense that they *force* one to adopt a view that is firmly, even wildly, against common sense. I don't think I'll ever have a decent reason to think that such-and-such a detailed response to a given paradox is correct. For instance, by my lights the presently existing public considerations regarding the Sorites paradox are in favor of epistemicism. But why on earth would I think that those considerations – the ones we have *today*, located in the *public* sphere – are good enough to point us in the right direction? I can't think of any good reason to think that; in fact, there are excellent reasons (not given here) to think that that's just plain false. In any case, I wondered whether I could justify my gut feeling that certain philosophical paradoxes refute portions of common sense – no matter what the correct solution was to those paradoxes. So, I tried to find that justification, with reference to several philosophical paradoxes. Like many philosophers familiar with paradoxes, I used to think of paradoxes as seemingly valid arguments from commonsensical premises to highly counterintuitive conclusions. So, I figured that the mere existence of the paradoxes proved that either a commonsensical premise is false, a seemingly valid argument is invalid, or a highly counterintuitive conclusion is true. As hinted at with the $\{C_1, C_2, \sim(C_1 \ \& \ C_2)\}$ scenario discussed earlier in this Introduction, now I see that that diagnosis misses some possibilities.

What the paradoxes have in common is that an exhaustive analysis of each of them reveals that any of its proposed solutions is philosophically counterintuitive, in a sense to be defined in Section 2. That's a nice thesis, but things get much more interesting when we pool these analyses together. When we do so, we find interesting metaphilosophical and epistemological insights on six topics:

- philosophical progress
- agreement in philosophy
- knockdown arguments in philosophy
- the wisdom of philosophical belief
- the epistemic status of metaphysics
- the power of philosophy to refute common sense

In Section 2, I briefly elaborate on those six topics. But if you are impatient to hear the *central* take-home lesson, which lies in the intersection of epistemology and metaphilosophy, here it is:

As I have pointed out, many philosophers think that philosophy never refutes common sense; many philosophers also think there are no knockdown arguments in nonformal philosophy. What would be extraordinary would be philosophical arguments that did both! However, that's what I argue for here: There are many arguments that (1) clearly belong to nonformal philosophy, (2) are knockdown, and (3) conclude that some violently counterintuitive claims are true; furthermore, once the typical philosopher is aware of the truth of that thesis, she should, in order to be wise, withhold judgment on a colossal number of claims, even highly commonsensical ones. Hence, a lesson of philosophy's success is that once the wise philosopher becomes aware of these facts, she will suspend judgment much more often than she once did. In that sense, we fall doxastic victim to our own argumentative success.

2 Our Six Topics

Philosophers have been complaining about metaphysics for a long time, claiming that it is bullshit when compared to most other areas of philosophy (e.g. Ladyman and Ross 2007). Even today, almost all of us encounter jabs at it, in conversation and on social media if not in print. Up until now, the metaphysician's best response has been: "Oh yeah? Let's see your response to such-and-such metaphysical problem, if you think metaphysics is bullshit." The critics and defenders are rarely impressed with the ensuing discussion, should there be any at all.

Philosophers have been complaining about the lack of philosophical progress for a long time (e.g. some of the papers in Blackford and Broderick 2020). Even today, almost all of us encounter jabs at it, in conversation and on social media if not in print. Most complainers are willing to admit that there are some forms of philosophical progress: new distinctions are discovered that are philosophically key, new problems are discovered, new theories are formulated, new arguments are constructed, new thought experiments are conceived, new fields are generated, and so on. These new things help us see deeper into certain topics, in ways that are hard to articulate non-metaphorically. But even if we grant all of those forms of progress, philosophical progress is anemic compared to scientific progress when it comes to getting substantive, positive truths that are answers to burning questions. It's not like we have solved many really big problems. If we had, then why the hell would we still be reading Aristotle and Kant for solutions instead of as historians only?

Philosophers have been complaining about the power of philosophy to refute common sense for a long time (e.g. Moore 1925; Lewis 1973; Fine 2001; Lycan 2001, 2019; Gupta 2006; Kelly 2008; Schaffer 2009). Even today, almost all of us encounter jabs at it, in conversation and on social media if not in print. These philosophers admit that science is up to the task, and some admit that formal philosophy is as well. The more modest ones are willing to admit that maybe, just maybe, philosophy can be transformed in some surprising way such that nonformal philosophy refutes common sense in the future. But up until now? No way. They think that even if Moore's response to the argument for skepticism was flawed, the *Moorean move* is reasonable when one is confronted with a philosophical attempt to refute common sense:

> One starts out believing P, where one is fully aware that P is utterly commonsensical. One next encounters what one recognizes to be a nonformal philosophical argument A against P. In response, one forms the belief B that *P is significantly more warranted than at least one of the premises of A*. One then retains P with little or no change in confidence even if one admits that one has not (yet) found any flaw in A. This retaining of P is done on the basis of B.

Philosophers have been complaining about the lack of agreement in philosophy regarding philosophically substantive claims for a long time (e.g. van Inwagen 2006; cf. Frances 2017). Even today, almost all of us encounter jabs at it, in conversation and on social media if not in print. All one needs to do is scan the results of the PhilPapers surveys to witness how we fail to reach agreement on just about anything philosophically substantive. This is utterly different from what we find in the sciences.

Philosophers have been complaining about the lack of knockdown (and nonformal) philosophical arguments for philosophically substantive claims for a long time (e.g. Lewis 1983; van Inwagen 2014; cf. Ballantyne 2014; Keller 2015; McGrath and Kelly 2017). Even today, almost all of us encounter jabs at it, in conversation and on social media if not in print. For one thing, if such arguments existed, there certainly wouldn't be so much disagreement on philosophically substantive claims. But, again, just look at the results of the PhilPapers surveys.

As much as philosophers like to complain about the comparative inadequacies of metaphysics, the failure of nonformal philosophy to refute common sense, the anemic nature of philosophical progress compared to that of science, the lack of agreement on substantive philosophical matters, and the failure to produce knockdown nonformal philosophical arguments for philosophically substantive claims, if my experience is at all representative, then what philosophers *really hate* is the idea that the typical wise philosopher should, epistemically if not professionally, suspend judgment on philosophical claims. Think about it: You work for years and years defending your niche position, defending it in multiple publications, and you're not epistemically allowed to even believe it? Are you serious?

What this means is that my theses in this Element will be resisted. I'm reminded of Franklin Roosevelt's address announcing the Second New Deal on October 31, 1936: "Never before in all our history have these forces been so united against one candidate as they stand today. They are unanimous in their hate for me – and I welcome their hatred." I'm joking.

In the Introduction, I asserted that we can prove philosophically counterintuitive results from analyses of philosophical problems – and we can do it without taking any stand on the solutions to any of those problems. In order to do this, we start by giving a logically exhaustive analysis of several traditional philosophical paradoxes. The analysis allows us to prove disjunctions that have a small number of disjuncts and have the following features:

- The arguments for the disjunctions are "knockdown" arguments, pretty much however one wants to precisify that notion in a reasonable manner.
- We philosophers are strongly disposed, after seeing the proofs, to agree that the disjunctions are true.
- Each disjunct is *philosophically counterintuitive*: If it is true, then a great many of our ordinary commonsensical beliefs and/or a significant portion of our most confidently held ordinary beliefs or belief-dispositions are false, or key philosophical ideas held by a large portion of philosophers are false. (More on this characterization in Section 4.)
- Once we philosophers are aware of the truth of the disjunctions, we realize that we have been *wildly* wrong about language, logic, truth, or ordinary empirical matters.
- Awareness of the truth of the disjunctions makes the typical wise philosopher suspect that she should not trust her judgment, in a profound manner.
- Once one is aware of the truth of the disjunctions, the typical philosopher must, in order to be wise, suspend judgment on an enormous number of claims, even many of the most certain ones.

As a bonus, the materials used to prove the disjunctions cast light on whether metaphysics is bullshit (it's not; in fact, in one key respect it is superior to some other areas of philosophy), what kind of substantive philosophical progress there is on particular philosophical claims (it exists, although in an unexpected form), and whether (nonformal) philosophy – instead of science – can refute common sense (yes).

3 How to Analyze a Philosophical Problem: The Sorites

Philosophical problems that stick around for centuries often fall into one of two classes. First, there are those that have multiple proposed solutions that are not *terribly* counterintuitive but we collectively have not figured out which solution is right. Second, there are the really hard problems: those that seem to *require* a highly counterintuitive solution but we haven't figured out which is true. Opinions will differ about which class a particular problem is a member of; relatedly, there will be loads of borderline cases. Despite those issues, there are obvious citizens of the second class. Aficionados of those problems usually take it for granted that any mature response to them will include a claim that is not mildly odd but highly counterintuitive.

This isn't a book on the Sorites paradox, even though I am going to analyze it. What is relevant about the paradox is the fact that, like many philosophical paradoxes, it can be used to prove what I call a *doxastically distressing disjunction*. To that end, consider the following SC claims ("S" for "sorites," "C" for "claim").

SC_1: Anyone worth less than \$1 (US) is (financially) poor.

SC_2: Either it's not the case that anyone worth less than \$1 is poor, or anyone worth less than \$2 is poor. (In other words, if everyone with less than \$1 is poor, then so is everyone with less than \$2.)[1]

SC_3: Either it's not the case that anyone worth less than \$2 is poor, or anyone worth less than \$3 is poor.

. . .

SC_{LAST}: It's not the case that anyone worth less than $\$10^{12}$ is poor.

On the face of it, the SCs are collectively inconsistent, since one can easily derive $\sim SC_{LAST}$ from the other SCs using simple inferences (more on that in this section).

This Element is not concerned with the solutions to Sorites or any other classic philosophical problem. I don't care what your favored solution is, I don't want to hear you blather on about it, and it won't matter to my arguments at all. (The harsh language, which will be repeated in what follows, is for both amusement and, more importantly, hard emphasis that the solutions to the paradoxes do not affect the arguments of this Element.) Instead, we are focusing on the philosophically significant consequences of these problems themselves, not specific proposed solutions to them.

There are exactly five possibilities with regard to the SCs: The first three collectively cover all the ways the conjunction of the SCs can be false and the last two cover the two ways it can be true ("S" for "sorites" and "D" for "disjunct," since I will be examining the disjunction of the five claims in what follows).

---

[1] Instead of disjunctions we could use material conditionals (e.g. "If anyone worth less than \$1 is poor, then anyone worth less than \$2 is poor"). I stick with disjunctions because many philosophers seem to be wary of material conditionals and I want to avoid those discussions.

SD_1: $\sim SC_1$

SD_2: $\sim SC_{LAST}$

SD_3: $\sim[SC_2 \ \& \ SC_3 \ \& \ \ldots \ \& \ SC_{LAST-1}]$

SD_4: $SC_1 \ \& \ SC_2 \ \& \ \ldots \ \& \ SC_{LAST}$ & there is no truth-preserving derivation to a contradiction

SD_5: $SC_1 \ \& \ SC_2 \ \& \ \ldots \ \& \ SC_{LAST}$ & there is a truth-preserving derivation to a contradiction

The reader can verify with mere sentential logic that the disjunction of the five SDs is true. Thus, *the disjunction of the five SDs is logically true.* (More on this alleged fact in Section 9.) This is not the doxastically distressing disjunction I referred to earlier in this section. We encounter that disjunction in Section 5.

Things are going to get complicated in what follows, so it's appropriate to give a sense of the road before us. There are the "sorites claims," the SCs. Then there are the "sorites disjuncts," the SDs. I will be focusing on the latter. I will argue that each SD is philosophically counterintuitive. You might think the conclusion of those arguments is simple: Since the disjunction of the five SDs is true (as pointed out in this section), and each is philosophically counterintuitive (Section 4), this proves that some philosophically counterintuitive claim is true (viz. one of the SDs). Unfortunately, that's not right; there are some linguistic complications that must be addressed (Section 4). But in Section 5 we will construct a "doxastically distressing disjunction" that is obviously true (given the arguments in Sections 3 and 4) and yet it's also obvious that each disjunct is philosophically counterintuitive; hence, we have a *philosophical* argument that is *knockdown* (in senses to be discussed in Section 9) and concludes that some *violently counterintuitive* claim is true. Section 6 will consider an objection, one that doesn't require any modification of the doxastically distressing disjunction. Sections 7 and 8 take the proof method that I used on the sorites and apply it to a couple of other paradoxes in order to generate a couple more doxastically distressing disjunctions. The rest of the Element formulates and defends my ten theses.

4 Each Disjunct Is Philosophically Counterintuitive

In this section, I examine only the *obvious, immediate* philosophically interesting consequences of each disjunct, SD_1–SD_5. I will not be arguing that any particular disjunct is true (or not true). Instead, my commentaries on the disjuncts have two purposes:

- articulate the obvious, immediate philosophically interesting consequences of the disjuncts
- prove that each disjunct is *philosophically counterintuitive*, pretty much no matter how one reasonably makes that notion precise so that it comes out useful.

One can precisify "philosophically counterintuitive" as follows: A claim is philosophically counterintuitive at a time if and only if (i) if the claim is true, then a great many of our ordinary commonsensical beliefs and/or a significant portion of our most confidently held ordinary beliefs or belief-dispositions are false, or (ii) if the claim is true, then key philosophical ideas held by a large portion of philosophers at that time are false. Under (i), we have claims such as "Mom knows you bought a motorcycle," "Kat believes global warming isn't happening," and "There are eight trees along the backyard property line." Under (ii), we have claims such as "Modus ponens is truth preserving," "No contradictions are true," "The fact that 'Bertrand Russell' refers is not a brute fact." Some claims might fall into both categories; it won't matter. I don't know if "philosophically counterintuitive" is the best term. "Philosophically significant" and "philosophically consequential" were considered. Set aside aptness of vocabulary. I will comment on this notion further in Section 12, addressing its philosophical significance (e.g. why should we care if a truth is "philosophically counterintuitive"?).

SD_1:   It's not the case that anyone with less than \$1 is poor.

It might seem fairly obvious that SD_1 is philosophically counterintuitive. It is saying that some people with virtually no money aren't poor. That's about as counterintuitive as a claim can get. It might not be as counterintuitive as "$2 + 2 = 576$" or "I am not conscious at all, in any sense whatsoever," but it's still highly counterintuitive. If it's not the case that anyone (today) with less than \$1 (US) is (financially) poor, then a great many of our ordinary commonsensical beliefs, or a significant portion of our most confidently held ordinary beliefs or belief-dispositions, are not true. Thus, SD_1 is philosophically counterintuitive.

There is, however, a way that this argument might be unsound. Suppose SD_1 is true, so "Anyone with less than \$1 is poor" isn't true as that sentence is used in this work of philosophy. Even so, perhaps that sentence is true when used in ordinary discourse. And if it is true in ordinary discourse, then its being false in philosophical discourse may not be nearly as counterintuitive. Just because SD_1 is false in this Element won't mean, necessarily, that a great many of our ordinary commonsensical beliefs, or a significant portion of our most confidently held ordinary beliefs or belief-dispositions, are not true.

This type of situation happens. For instance, ordinary discourse employing "miracle," "conscious," "believe," and "justified" might not match up with philosophical discourse using the same terms, since the two discourses often (not always) employ different relevant meanings (i.e. ones that change truth-value even in extensional sentential contexts). The following sentences, appearing in philosophical discourse, should strike a philosopher as having a real chance at being false:

If her belief was not justified, then "Her belief was justified" isn't true in ordinary discourse.
If there are no miracles, then "There are miracles" isn't true in ordinary discourse.

When I argued that SD_1 is philosophically counterintuitive, it's arguable that I tacitly employed a similar premise in my argument:

1. If SD_1 is true, then "It's not the case that anyone with less than \$1 is poor" is true in the discourse I am using right now in this Element.
2. If that sentence is true in the discourse I'm using right now in this Element, then it's true in ordinary discourse.
3. If it's true in ordinary discourse, then a great many of our ordinary common-sensical beliefs, or a significant portion of our most confidently held ordinary beliefs or belief-dispositions, are not true.
4. Hence, by (1)–(3), if SD_1 is true, then a great many of our ordinary commonsensical beliefs, or a significant portion of our most confidently held ordinary beliefs or belief-dispositions, are not true.

Sure enough, if premise (2) is true, then SD_1 is philosophically counterintuitive (since (1) and (3) are true and {(1)–(3)} entails (4), as the conditionals (1)–(3) are material). But is (2) true?

I suppose that if one is sentimental enough, and in the sentimentality has a certain direction so to speak, one might be tempted by the idea that philosophical discourse is quite different from ordinary discourse: more sophisticated, more elegant, urbane, almost divine, ontologically and explanatorily fit, and extraordinarily charming, good-looking, and sexually impressive. Or perhaps it goes in the other direction: philosophical discourse is ill-suited for ever finding truth, hopelessly ambiguous, ugly, smelly, and crude. Joking aside, though, there are five excellent reasons for thinking that (2) is true.

First, there aren't any problematic terms here similar to "miracle" or "justified"; hence, that particular reason to be suspicious of (2) fails to apply. Second, I am explicitly saying – right now, if you like – that I am using, in this Element, ordinary English – unless, of course, I *supplement* it with philosophical jargon, which clearly doesn't appear in the SCs. Third, there are good reasons, offered by Timothy Williamson (forthcoming; cf. van Inwagen 2014), for thinking that philosophers are using ordinary English in their discussions of the ontology of the everyday world. Fourth, even if there is a language typically used in the "ontology room" that makes "Anyone with less than $1 is poor" express a proposition truth-conditionally different from the one it expresses in ordinary English, I am explicitly saying that I'm not using that philosophical language here and I am using ordinary English – and such a proclamation should shift the linguistic interpretation accordingly. Fifth, there doesn't seem to be anything *preventing* me from using "Anyone with less than $1 is poor" with its ordinary meaning. Philosophers who think there is a separate language, "ontologese," don't think that a philosopher is *incapable* of using ordinary English when using sentences that *could* be used in ontologese. In short, there is little good reason to think (2) isn't true, and there is excellent reason to think it is true.

But what if I simply am *unable*, in this Element, to use ordinary English in my analysis of the SCs no matter what I say or do? Amazingly enough, it doesn't matter for my purposes in this Element. Suppose that the argument of the previous paragraph is unsound and (2) isn't true, so "Anyone with less than $1 is poor" has different truth-values in ordinary discourse and in this Element, despite the fact that SC_1 is a sentence of perfectly ordinary English (however one wants to spell that out) and I have insisted that I am using ordinary English.

I still win. That is because (2)'s being false – despite the lack of obviously problematic terms and my explicit insistence that I am using ordinary English here *even if* there is some other, philosophical, language available – would mean that most of us have been wildly wrong about linguistic interpretation. And that would be a philosophically counterintuitive result. *You* might not find it counterintuitive. That's irrelevant. For arguments concerning the significance of these arguments (instead of their soundness), see Sections 9–12, especially Section 12.

Hence, I am *not* claiming or even faintly suggesting that (2) is true, although that's what I suspect is the case. Instead, I'm saying that we have a philosophically counterintuitive result whether or not (2) is true.

In sum, here's my argument, with symbolization guidance regarding the entailments:

a. If SD_1 is true in ordinary discourse, then a great many of our ordinary commonsensical beliefs and/or a significant portion of our most confidently held ordinary beliefs or belief-dispositions are false. $(A \supset Z1)$

b. If (i) SD_1 is not true in ordinary discourse but (ii) SD_1 is true in this Element, (iii) I have instructed that tokens of SD_1 in this Element belong to ordinary

English (even if they could belong to another language), and (iv) SD_1 does not contain any philosophical jargon not in ordinary English, then key philosophical ideas held by many contemporary philosophers are false. [$(\sim A \& B \& C \& D) \supset Z2$]

c. I have instructed that tokens of SD_1 in this Element belong to ordinary English (even if they could belong to another language), and SD_1 does not contain any philosophical jargon not in ordinary English. (C & D)

d. Hence, by (a)–(c), if SD_1 is true in this Element, then either (i) a great many of our ordinary commonsensical beliefs and/or a significant portion of our most confidently held ordinary beliefs or belief-dispositions are false or (ii) key philosophical ideas held by many contemporary philosophers are false. $B \supset (Z1 \vee Z2)$

e. Hence, by (d) and the definition of "philosophically counterintuitive," SD_1 is philosophically counterintuitive.

In the arguments that follow, we will occasionally encounter other premises like (2) from a few paragraphs back. Each has the form "If 'S' is true in the discourse I'm using right now in this Element, then it's true in ordinary discourse." I will call them *bridge premises* since they purport to bridge the alleged gap between my sentences in this Element and ordinary discourse.

SD_2:　Anyone with less than $\$10^{12}$ is poor.

It might seem fairly obvious that SD_2 is philosophically counterintuitive. It is saying that everyone is poor, given that everyone (today) has less than $\$10^{12}$. That's about as counterintuitive as a claim can get.

As with SD_1, there is another possibility: "Anyone with less than $\$10^{12}$ is poor" is true as that sentence is used in this work of philosophy but it's not true when used in ordinary life. That is, the relevant bridge premise is false. But this is highly unlikely, for the same five reasons I gave above regarding the bridge premise for SD_1. And even if the bridge premise for SD_2 is false, this result would be philosophically counterintuitive as well for the same reason in SD_1. Thus, we have a proof that SD_2 is philosophically counterintuitive. The argument can be set out with (a)–(e) as above with merely substituting "SD_2" for "SD_1."

It's worth keeping in mind that sorites arguments turn on a great many kinds of terms. They need not use terms with obvious context dependency such as "is poor," "is tall," etc. Sorites arguments can turn on predicates such as "is a pumpkin." For instance, we can do a sorites series on a particular, ordinary, token utterance of "There is a pumpkin by the tree," by proceeding through a series of cases that diminish the pumpkin microscopically starting from its top (so the sentence starts out true and ends up false; I will examine this case a couple more times in what follows). We can even use proper names such as "Bertrand Russell": use "Bertrand Russell exists" and consider a sorites series starting from a case in which he clearly exists at a certain time and proceed step by step to a case in which he clearly does not exist (e.g. fiddle with the physical makeup of his origin). Or we can employ other kinds of terms. There are various ways to alter the cases, temporally or, alternatively, counterfactually.

Hence, there is an *enormous* number and variety of sorites series. So, if either SD_1 or SD_2 is true, the consequences will be massive.

SD_3: For some integral N ($1 < N < 10^{12}$), anyone worth less than \$(N − 1) is poor but someone worth less than \$N is not poor.

Most philosophers are less familiar with SD_3 than with either of SD_1 and SD_2. So, I will go over it in more detail.

Suppose SD_3 is true, so for some N, anyone worth less than \$(N − 1) is poor but someone worth less than \$N is not poor. Given the obvious empirical claims about the diversity in financial worth in the world (almost all of us are disposed to think that for most small intervals of net worth, there are at least a couple of people whose net worth falls into that interval), it follows from SD_3 that

(*) There actually are a couple of people only dollars apart but one is poor while the other is not.

Furthermore, even if in actuality there aren't two people that close to the alleged cutoff, SD_3 requires this:

(**) It is easily possible for there to be a couple of people only a dollar apart but one is poor while the other is not.

Now keep in mind the point made regarding SD_2 that sorites arguments can be applied to a great many ordinary claims. Hence, if SD_3 is true, then a staggering number and variety of claims very similar to (*) and (**) are true. The collection of these claims shows that clause (i) of the characterization of philosophically counterintuitive is satisfied: "If the claim is true, then a great many of our ordinary commonsensical beliefs and/or a significant portion of our most confidently held ordinary beliefs or belief-dispositions are false" (in particular, the bit about belief-dispositions).

You may suspect that philosophers familiar with the Sorites do not have beliefs or belief-dispositions inconsistent with either (*) or (**) (see Doulas and Welchance 2021). Of course, they used to, but maybe today things are different. If so, then perhaps SD_3 *no longer* satisfies clause (i) even though it once did. I will respond to this objection in Section 12.

We can also see that clause (ii) of the characterization of philosophical counterintuitiveness, "If the claim is true, then key philosophical ideas held by a large portion of philosophers at that time are false," is satisfied. Here's why:

If SD_3 is true, then "is poor" has a stunningly precise meaning, one that fits exactly one of these two people, who are just dollars (even cents) apart. But how on earth did "is poor" *acquire* such an amazingly discriminating meaning, applying to just one of a pair of people with virtually the same amount of money? No one has offered even the faintest plausible story, and there is good reason to think none is forthcoming. So, if SD_3 is true, then key philosophical ideas held by a large portion of philosophers are false.

With some work, one could offer a *stipulation* regarding "is poor" so that under the resulting interpretation "For some integral N $(1 < N < 10^{12})$, anyone worth less than \$(N − 1) is poor but anyone worth less than \$N is not poor" is true and not philosophically counterintuitive. However, that fact doesn't suggest for an instant that the sentence *already*, in the actual world today prior to our stipulation, has an accurate interpretation with that consequence.

If you accept SD_3, then you surely have to wonder what shocking falsehoods there are about language and thought that you have hitherto presumed. Given time, you could grow comfortable accepting many other comparably outrageous ideas, such as the one that there can be two perfectly ordinary pumpkinish things that differ in one chemical atom – out of around 10^{30} total, so they are literally about 99.99999999999999999999999999 percent overlapping – but only one of which is a pumpkin (see Section 8 for elaboration). Or the other wild idea that a perfectly ordinary token of "The restaurant is a short walk from here" (said to a visiting friend, say) goes from true to not true in the space of a yoctometer (10^{-24} m). It's great that you have managed to accept linguistic miracles; it's impressive that you have gotten over your *previous* discomfort with some counterintuitive claims. But then, why think your *continuing* discomfort with any *other* counterintuitive claim isn't misguided as well?

There are two points here. First, there's the one just made: If I'm wrong that of two pumpkinish things that are 99.99999999999999999999999999 percent overlapping, the one with 10^{30} atoms not being a pumpkin while the one with those 10^{30} atoms plus one more being a pumpkin, if my ordinary words and thoughts have such incredibly exact meanings, then I could be wrong about a great many commonsensical claims about meaning.

Second, the grounds of meaning are made positively magical, relative to what philosophers have typically supposed. After all, who would have thought that if one puts into one pot all the factors that help fix linguistic meanings that pot would give to a perfectly ordinary utterance token of "The restaurant is a short walk from here" – an utterance token made in certain highly specific, perfectly ordinary, circumstances, so we avoid speaker contextual issues – a truth condition that can distinguish two situations a yoctometer apart? If someone who used "short walk" in the distant past had, counterfactually, farted during their utterance, or had a sore little toe that made him not want to make the walk to his favorite restaurant, would a slightly different middle SC have been untrue, so the cutoff for the restaurant sentence token ended up at $10^{26} + 117.11111$ ym instead of $10^{26} + 117.11112$ ym? Or stick with the pumpkin case: How on earth did an ordinary, everyday token of "There is a pumpkin by the tree" acquire a truth condition so that the thing A with 10^{30} atoms doesn't satisfy it even though thing B that is identical with A but with one more atom does satisfy it? Or focus on the financial worth case: Jack's net worth is $1 less than Jill's but she isn't poor even though he is. No one has the slightest remotely plausible idea *how* perfectly ordinary token utterances of ordinary sentences such as those could ever acquire such utterly miraculous discriminating truth conditions.

The alternative idea that these sharp cutoff facts are marvelous yet brute, so there is no pot of things that fix meanings, would show, once again, that we are wildly wrong about meaning and thought. There may be brute facts! That's fine. But surely the sharp cutoff facts for perfectly ordinary tokens of "There is a pumpkin by the tree" and "The restaurant is a short walk from here" aren't among them.

Let me be perfectly clear: I'm *not* arguing, asserting, assuming, or even faintly suggesting that SD_3 is false (regarding my commentary on SD_3, see Horgan 1997 and Williamson 1997a, 1997b for discussion). I am not arguing against epistemicism, brute linguistic facts, or any related view. So, if you advocate one of those views, stop complaining. I'm only presenting a proof that SD_3 is philosophically counterintuitive: If it's true, then the second condition for "philosophically counterintuitive" is satisfied. (Earlier in this section we saw that the first condition is satisfied. Frankly, all we need is one half satisfied in order for my arguments to go through.) Finally, this thesis of mine is not in any tension with the claim that SD_3 *should*, normatively, not be philosophically counterintuitive; the same holds for my commentary on the other disjuncts.

To reach those conclusions, I used the supposition that it's highly counterintuitive that, for some integral N ($1 < N < 10^{12}$), anyone worth less than $(N − 1)$ is poor but someone worth less than $N is not poor. And here, I'm assuming that if "For some integral N ($1 < N < 10^{12}$), anyone worth less than $(N − 1)$ is poor but someone worth less than $N is not poor" is true in this Element, then it's true in ordinary discourse; that is the relevant bridge premise. As with SD_1 and SD_2, there are no philosophically troublesome terms here such as "justified," "conscious," "miracle," or "belief"; I have insisted that I am using ordinary English and so on. Hence, if the sentence has different truth-values in ordinary and philosophical discourse, then we have been wildly wrong about interpretation. And if that's so, that is a philosophically counterintuitive result.

In sum, here's my argument, again with guidance regarding the entailments:

a. If SD_3 is true in ordinary discourse, then key philosophical ideas held by many contemporary philosophers are false (viz. ones about meaning determination, brute facts, etc.). $(A \supset Z)$

b. If SD_3 is not true in ordinary discourse but is true in this Element, I have instructed that tokens of SD_3 in this Element belong to ordinary English (even if they could belong to another language), and SD_3 does not contain any philosophical jargon not in ordinary English, then key philosophical ideas held by many contemporary philosophers are false (viz. ones about interpretation). $[(\sim A \ \& \ B \ \& \ C \ \& \ D) \supset Z]$

c. I have instructed that tokens of SD_3 in this Element belong to ordinary English (even if they could belong to another language), and SD_3 does not contain any philosophical jargon not in ordinary English. $(C \ \& \ D)$

d. Hence, by (a)–(c), if SD_3 is true in this Element, then key philosophical ideas held by many contemporary philosophers are false. $(B \supset Z)$

e. Hence, by (d) and clause (ii) of the definition of "philosophically counterintuitive," SD_3 is philosophically counterintuitive.

f. If SD_3 is true in ordinary discourse, then a great many other, very similar claims (from other sorites series) are true and they collectively show that a significant portion of our most confidently held ordinary beliefs or belief-dispositions are false. $(A \supset Y)$

g. Hence, by (f) and clause (i) of the definition of "philosophically counterintuitive," SD_3 is philosophically counterintuitive.

SD_4: $SC_1 \ \& \ SC_2 \ \& \ \ldots \ \& \ SC_{LAST} \ \&$ there is no truth-preserving derivation to a contradiction.

If SD_4 is true, then all the SCs are true and yet it's not the case that $\sim SC_{LAST}$ – despite the apparent fact that the latter can be straightforwardly derived from the SCs using one of the simplest inference rules of mere sentential logic applied to non-paradoxical sentences: P, $(\sim P \ v \ Q)$; hence, Q.

There are exactly two ways the obvious derivation from the (all but the final) SCs to $\sim SC_{LAST}$ can fail to be truth-preserving. First, it relies on a sentential inference rule that isn't truth-preserving when applied to the SCs. Second, the inference rules in the obvious derivation are truth-preserving but do not apply to the SCs because the middle SCs aren't disjunctions. Those are the only possibilities.

Under the first option, SD_4 is *not* saying that the SCs have some logical structure so that the rule "P, $(\sim P \ v \ Q)$; hence, Q" doesn't apply to them (which would mean the middle SCs aren't disjunctions, despite appearances). Instead, it's saying that although the rule does apply to them in exactly the simple way we have always thought, the rule itself is not truth-preserving. Hence, even though both

1. "Either it's not the case that anyone worth less than $10,000 is poor, or anyone worth less than $10,001 is poor"; and
2. "Anyone worth less than $10,000 is poor"

are true *and* the first disjunct of (1) is indeed the negation of (2),

3. "Anyone worth less than $10,001 is poor"

isn't true (using $10,000 for the sake of illustration). If that's the way things are, then we have been wildly wrong about the most elementary logic. If we have been wrong about how this sentential (not higher-order! not modal! not even predicate!) rule "P, (~P v Q); thus, Q" is truth-preserving when applied to perfectly familiar and simple sentences (1)–(3), then we have a philosophically counterintuitive result. If it matters to you, the sentences (1)–(3) aren't paradoxical ones, such as those that generate Liar problems.

An oddity: If we reject the truth-preservingness of "P, (~P v Q); thus, Q," then can we even accept that the disjunction of the five sorites SDs is true? Why should we, once we have given up on one of the simplest rules of sentential logic? Earlier in this section, I stated that the disjunction of the five SDs is logically true, but of course I was assuming the reader would go along with me in accepting the elementary rules of inference that would be used in the relevant proof. I return to this issue in Section 9.

The second way SD$_4$ could be true: The inference rule in question is truth-preserving but doesn't apply to the SCs, because *the middle SCs aren't disjunctions*. That is, this claim isn't a disjunction:

> Either it's not the case that anyone worth less than $1 is poor, or anyone worth less than $2 is poor.

But if that's true, then of course most of us (all of us?) have been wildly wrong about interpretation, for even the simplest sentences of natural language. Again, a philosophically counterintuitive result. On top of that, we have an "oddity" similar to the one mentioned a paragraph back: If we are going to say that the middle SCs are not, contrary to appearances, disjunctions, then why think the elementary rules of inference apply to the five Ds in order to generate a proof of their disjunction?

There's no implicit assumption in the previous paragraphs that our formal logic devices can "fully capture" sentences of natural language, whatever "fully capture" is supposed to mean here. Just look again at (1) and (2): How in God's name could they be true while (3) is false *and* the rule "P, (~P v Q); thus, Q" is truth-preserving – which is what this second way of making SD_4 true requires? Is the advocate of the second way saying that (1) is not even a disjunction? If so, then what could it be? Or is he saying that (1) is a disjunction but miraculously its first disjunct isn't the negation of (2)? What is *stopping* (2) from being negated and made into a disjunct in (1)? This is the simplest sentential logic there is, not anything fancy. You don't have to worship logic in order to find philosophically counterintuitive this second way that SD_4 could be true.

Hence, the counterintuitive nature of SD_4 comes from its disjunctive consequences: Either the elementary inference-type in question is truth-preserving but we have badly misunderstood the meanings of the sentences (so the rule is fine but doesn't apply to the SCs) or we have understood the meanings of the sentences but the inference-type isn't truth-preserving (the meanings are fine but the rule isn't). (Or *both* the rule and meanings aren't fine.) Hence, the truth of SD_4 would have profound implications for either (*) how we understand linguistic meaning, since the SCs are quite simple sentences but we don't understand them, or (**) how we understand logic, since the unsound inference is exceedingly simple and seemingly truth-preserving. And recall the point made earlier in this section: There is an enormous number and variety of instances of the sorites, so (*) and (**) go far beyond the SCs in my illustration.

Hence, we have proven that SD_4 is philosophically counterintuitive. I don't want to repeat myself (too much), but notice that the proof never says that SD_4 or either of its disjunctive consequences is false. If we wanted to assert that, we would have to give up "proven" and replace it with "argued."

SD_5: SC_1 & SC_2 & ... & SC_{LAST} & there is a truth-preserving derivation to a contradiction.

If SD_5 is true, then anyone with less than 10^{12} is poor and it's not the case that anyone with less than 10^{12} is poor. This result is counterintuitive for two reasons. First, it's first conjunct, "Anyone with less than 10^{12} is poor," is philosophically counterintuitive for the same reasons SD_2 was. Second, it's obviously contradictory, which is philosophically counterintuitive as well, especially since SC_{LAST} isn't even a paradoxical sentence (e.g. from the Liar paradox).

Since there is an enormous variety and number of sorites series, if we think the one I've used in this section reveals a pair of true contradictory claims, then an enormous variety and number of other pairs of contradictory claims are true too (even if we adopt a paraconsistent logic, so that it's not the case that everything follows from just one contradiction). Hence, if SD$_5$ is true, then we have true contradictions galore.

5 A Doxastically Distressing Disjunction: The Sorites

The proofs of the previous section, combined with the premise that the disjunction of the five SDs is true (not: logically true), amounts to a proof of the disjunction of the following seven claims:

- "Someone with less than one dollar isn't poor" is true in ordinary discourse. (First disjunctive consequence of SD$_1$; second one is in the last bullet point.)
- "Everyone is poor" is true in ordinary discourse. (First disjunctive consequence of SD$_2$; second one is in the last bullet point; this is also one of the consequences of SD$_5$.)
- "There are a couple of people only dollars apart but one is poor while the other is not" is true in ordinary discourse. (First disjunctive consequence of SD$_3$, relying on the rough premise that, for most small intervals of net worth, there are people both of whom have a net worth in that interval; the second disjunctive consequence is in the last bullet point.)
- At least one of the simplest sentential inference rules isn't truth-preserving when applied to pairs of very simple sentences. (First disjunctive consequence of SD$_4$.)
- At least some of the middle SCs aren't even disjunctions. (Second disjunctive consequence of SD$_4$.)
- There are a great many true contradictions coming from ordinary sentences (not weird, liar-type ones), even assuming a paraconsistent logic. (One of the two consequences of SD$_5$.)
- At least some of the sentences expressing SD$_1$–SD$_3$ are true in this Element but false in ordinary discourse, despite not containing philosophical jargon and contrary to my explicit interpretative instructions. (Second disjunctive consequence of each of SD$_1$–SD$_3$, relying on the conjunctive premise after the comma.)

Given the stipulation for "philosophically counterintuitive," it's clear that the first three bullet points satisfy the first clause and the rest satisfy the second clause. Here is the stipulation again:

Def: A claim is *philosophically counterintuitive* at a time = (i) if the claim is true, then a great many of our ordinary commonsensical beliefs and/or a significant portion of our most confidently held ordinary beliefs or belief-dispositions are false, or (ii) if the claim is true, then key philosophical ideas held by a large portion of philosophers at that time are false.

Hence, we have proved that each of the seven bullet points is philosophically counterintuitive. Thus, the true disjunction of the bullet points entails that there is a philosophically counterintuitive truth. And we have used just philosophical argument to prove this result. There is an objection to those arguments, which I consider in the next section, but it won't negatively affect matters.

To have a vocabulary for generalizing beyond the Sorites, we offer four useful stipulations (not claims).

Def: R is a *philosophical paradox* = R is a plurality of claims C_1–C_n such that upon consistent disambiguation (i) each C_i comes from the same philosophical problem, (ii) each C_i is individually highly plausible, (iii) it is highly plausible that there is a truth-preserving derivation from the Cs to a contradiction, and (iv) no proper sub-plurality of R satisfies (i)–(iii).

We include the bit about disambiguation in order to make sure that a philosophical problem that fits the four conditions isn't a pseudo-problem. For example, the three sentences "We have mental processes," "If something is mental, then it's not physical," and "We are entirely physical" each have interpretations that are highly plausible. For the sake of a clean example, pretend that, outside of philosophical discourse, occurrences of "mental" usually (not always) have a truth-conditional contribution such that "x is mental" requires the truth of "x isn't physical" (so in this scenario "mental" is unlike terms such as "hydrogen," for which deference to experts is prevalent). Pretend also that in philosophical discourse "mental" has no such connection to "not physical." The three sentences fail to generate a paradox because upon consistent disambiguation – so we interpret "mental" univocally in the first two sentences – at least one of the Cs is highly contentious. So, clause (ii) of the stipulation for "philosophical paradox" is not satisfied.

We add clause (iv) in an attempt to make sure R doesn't include anything irrelevant to the philosophical problem it is intended to capture. For instance, we should not add "Some people are neither poor nor not poor" to SC_1–SC_{LAST}, since the current SCs are all that are needed to produce the derivation to a contradiction. As an alternative to (iv), we could just say "Do not include anything irrelevant in R."

As you might suspect, we intend that many if not all of the traditional philosophical paradoxes satisfy the stipulation's four conditions. If they don't, then modify the stipulation accordingly; this is a mere detail. For me anyway, part of the beauty and profundity of paradoxes is that they can often be formulated in such a way as to satisfy (i)–(iv) – a feature that is not true of discourse on many other philosophical problems. Two more definitions:

Def: C is a *component of philosophical paradox* R = C is exactly one of paradox R.

Def: X is the *Disjunctive Analysis, DA, of philosophical paradox* R = X is the disjunction of the negation of each component of paradox R, the conjunction of the components of R plus the claim that there is a truth-preserving derivation from R to a contradiction, and the conjunction of the components of R plus the claim that there is no truth-preserving derivation from R to a contradiction.

For the Sorites, the DA is the disjunction of $(10^{12} + 3)$ claims: the negations of the $(10^{12} + 1)$ SCs, SD_4, and SD_5. More generally, if there are n components of paradox R, then there are $(n + 2)$ disjuncts of R's DA. The disjunction of the five SDs is of course logically equivalent to the DA for the Sorites.

DAs are apparently logical truths that serve as stepping stones to what turns out to be the key disjunctive truths:

Def: X is a *Consequence Disjunction, CD, of philosophical paradox* R = X is a disjunction of obvious, immediate philosophically relevant consequences of each of the disjuncts of the Disjunctive Analysis of paradox R.

For the Sorites, one CD is the disjunction of the seven bullet points preceding these four definitions. I can't think of a solid reason for the idea that a given paradox must have *just one* CD, although in order to be sure of the truth of the CD we restrict ourselves to the *obvious, immediate* consequences of each disjunct of the corresponding DA (as illustrated by my arguments leading to the CD for the Sorites). We also focus on the consequences that are philosophically interesting and relevant (e.g. I suppose "1 = 1" is an "obvious, immediate" consequence of almost everything, but it's hardly both philosophically relevant and interesting).

Consider "Either type identity theory is true or not true." I suppose there are some philosophers who find the first disjunct highly counterintuitive; and the same could be said for a quite different group of philosophers vis-à-vis the second disjunct. Does that mean it's actually easy to construct obviously true disjunctions each disjunct of which is philosophically counterintuitive? And doesn't that mean that the CDs I am focusing on are not that special?

No. It should go without saying that the disjuncts of the sorites CD are far, far more counterintuitive than those for the type identity disjunction. Further, for most philosophers, *all* the disjuncts are counterintuitive. It is not that easy to find disjunctions as surprising and significant as the CD ones.

So, we have two disjunctions: the DA one, which is logically true (unless we have made a grave mistake; see Section 9), and the CD one, which is not. As we will see, other philosophical problems can be used to prove similar pairs of disjunctions. For reasons given in Section 9, the CD is more important than the DA. Since each CD disjunct is philosophically counter-intuitive, we have *doxastically distressing disjunctions* (the CDs). Hence, I will focus on the CDs in what follows since they are the key to the epistemology of paradoxes.

6 How Semantic Complexity Does and Does Not Matter

The proof of the CD for the Sorites is complete, but the proof that each disjunct is philosophically counterintuitive is not. I complete the proof here by considering a clever linguistic objection. This section is probably best skipped on a first pass through the Element.

There are two issues to cover, one simple and one tricky. The simple one won't matter to my theses, but since it is one that often occurs to people, it is worth going over.

In order to derive "Anyone worth less than $\$10^{12}$ is poor" from the sorites SCs, or even univocally evaluate the individual SCs at all, we ensure that "anyone," "is worth," and "is poor" are univocal throughout the SCs so the derivation goes through in the usual way. (Strictly speaking, equivocation is fine as long as we still apparently reach inconsistency, but the most straightforward way to get there is to avoid equivocation.) There often are contextualist factors that need to be monitored in order to achieve univocality. For instance, do we mean with our use of "poor" poor for an unmarried 25-year-old living on her own in Manhattan in 2020, a 55-year-old with a spouse and four young children living in Dhaka in 1956, or what? In order to preserve univocality throughout the SCs we can, if we like, choose a particular "meaning" (e.g. comparison class and other factors) and use it in each SC. We can make this explicit by replacing "anyone" in the SCs with something like "any adult person permanently residing in Queens, New York in 1999 who is living on her own with no dependents" (or something more complicated; it won't matter). Similarly, we can precisify "is worth $N" with something involving a particular measure of net worth. Or we can quantify over a small set of closely similar measures. Or, what is easier, we can choose a particular conversational context and use it to fix meanings ("by my uses of 'poor', I meant whatever those folks over there meant in their ordinary, everyday conversation in ordinary English"), without offering any elaboration.

Independently of that matter, there is nothing stopping us from using "is poor" and "anyone" univocally.

When thinking about semantic complexities, it's worth keeping in mind a point I made in Section 4: Sorites arguments need not turn on terms with *obvious* context dependency such as "is poor." They can turn on predicates such as "is a pumpkin" or names such as "Bertrand Russell."

There is a way to get rid of contextual issues more plainly. Consider an alternative sorites series centering on a perfectly ordinary (given the context) token utterance of the sentence S "The restaurant is a short walk from here" such that: S_1 is a situation-type with respect to it's as certain as it ever gets that S is true, the neighboring S_N/S_{N+1} situations differ in just a minuscule difference in distance with respect to the restaurant, and S_{HUGE} has the restaurant as far away as you like, so it's obvious that S isn't true when evaluated with respect to S_{HUGE}. Now consider this collection of claims.

- S is true when evaluated with respect to S_1.
- Either S isn't true when evaluated with respect to S_1, or S is true when evaluated with respect to S_2.
  ...
- Either S isn't true when evaluated with respect to S_{HUGE-1}, or S is true when evaluated with respect to S_{HUGE}.
- It's not the case that S is true when evaluated with respect to S_{HUGE}.

In this case, we take a *token* utterance, with its contextual factors fixed, and assess it with respect to a sorites series. There is no contextual variation to deal with.

That's the straightforward semantic matter. I think it is relatively obvious there is no obstacle here to the arguments of the previous sections. There is another semantic complexity matter that is trickier, although it won't change the thesis that each CD disjunct is philosophically counterintuitive.

A critic of that thesis says that if we interpret the disjunction univocally, and of course accurately (using an interpretation that really does apply to the sentences in ordinary discourse), then of course I'm right that there must be a true disjunct under that interpretation (since the disjunction is true under any univocal and accurate interpretation; mere sentential logic proves it). However, she continues, it turns out that any true disjunct isn't philosophically counterintuitive. Sure, she says, each disjunct is counterintuitive under *some* accurate interpretation – exactly as I pointed out in Section 4. Indeed, that's why most philosophers think the Sorites paradox is a hard philosophical problem. But, she goes on, if we interpret the disjunction accurately and univocally, then any true disjunct will fail to be counterintuitive under *that* interpretation. Roughly put, there are two accurate interpretations available, I_1 and I_2, and although SD_3, say, is counterintuitive under I_1 (and that's the interpretation that makes the paradox seem like a real paradox), it's true only under I_2, which fails to make it counterintuitive. Hence, my objector is saying that there are semantic complexities that prove that *there is no accurate and univocal way of interpreting the disjunction such that it comes out true* and *has a true and philosophically counterintuitive disjunct*.

Call that the *Semantic Complexity objection*. Stated exactly, it makes two claims.

a. There is a disjunct SD_X and accurate and univocal interpretation I of the disjunction such that SD_X is true under I. That is, there is an accurate way of interpreting the disjunction of the five SDs so that at least one of them is true.
b. For any disjunct SD and accurate and univocal interpretation I of the disjunction, if I makes SD true, then SD is not philosophically counterintuitive under I. That is, no true disjunct is philosophically counterintuitive.

So, the objection entails that some sorites disjunct is true under some accurate interpretation but so interpreted it isn't philosophically counterintuitive, despite appearances to the contrary. And that result is supposed to take the wind out of the problem's sails, so to speak.

I have three comments on the Semantic Complexity objection. Eventually, I will be arguing that (b) is false when applied to the Sorites paradox.

First, the objection is at least *initially* plausible for some philosophical problems, ones in which there *might* be subtle contextual issues at the heart of the matter. For that reason alone, it is well worth taking the objection seriously. Let me explain the objection further, using a relevant example.

Obviously, "I am here now or it's not the case that I am here now" expresses a logical truth only if it's interpreted appropriately, due to the indexicals. A little more interestingly, the same holds for "Michelle is tall or it's not the case that Michelle is tall," this time due to the gradable adjective "is tall" (e.g. tall with respect to what?). More to the point, the same *might* hold for "Jan knows she has two woolly mammoths or it's not the case that Jan knows she has two woolly mammoths," even though it's not solely due to either indexicals or, arguably, gradable adjectives but something else complicated about "knows."

To see how this might matter to the analysis of philosophical problems, consider a simplified presentation of the Skepticism paradox.

A. If Jo knows that she has two woolly mammoths, then she is in a position to know that she isn't a mere brain in a vat.

B. It's not the case that Jo is in a position to know that she's not a mere brain in a vat.

C. Jo knows that she has two woolly mammoths.

Unlike you or me, it's completely clear that Jo has two woolly mammoths as pets. One can generate a logically true disjunction from those claims, using what I did with the sorites as a guide.

E_1: ~A

E_2: ~B

E_3: ~C

E_4: A & B & C & there is no truth-preserving derivation to a contradiction

E_5: A & B & C & there is a truth-preserving derivation to a contradiction

Of course, the disjunction of the five Es is logically true, just like how the disjunction of the five SDs is logically true. However, it's at least plausible that there are at least two *accurate*, univocal ways of interpreting the disjuncts: a "low-stakes" interpretation and a "high-stakes" interpretation (see Rysiew 2021). If we stick to a "low-stakes" accurate and univocal interpretation of the whole disjunction, then it's plausible that E_2 is true (so "Jo is in a position to know that she's not a mere brain in a vat" is true) but not counterintuitive. If we stick to a "high-stakes" accurate and univocal interpretation, then it's plausible that E_3 is true (so "Jo doesn't know that she has two woolly mammoths" is true) but not counterintuitive. Hence, although there is a disjunct E and accurate and univocal interpretation I such that E is true under I, *under no accurate interpretation is there a true disjunct that is counterintuitive*.

I am *not* endorsing that view. I'm just pointing out that the critic's Semantic Complexity objection has at least some plausibility for some philosophy problems.

Therefore, the Semantic Complexity objection might show, for *some* philosophical problems, that there is no interpretation of the corresponding disjunction that is accurate and univocal, that makes the disjunction true, and for which even one true disjunct is philosophically counterintuitive. And that would strongly suggest that the truth of the disjunction isn't nearly as significant as it initially seemed. That's my first, and conciliatory, comment on the objection.

Second, however, I fail to see the slightest reason to think that the objection applies to the Sorites paradox even if it applies to the Skepticism paradox (more on the latter at the end of this section). As noted, the Semantic Complexity objection entails that, for any sorites disjunct SD, any accurate and univocal interpretation of the disjunction that makes SD come out true won't make it counterintuitive – and yet, the objection admits that at least one disjunct is really true under some accurate and univocal interpretation of the disjunction. It follows that, in order for the objection to disarm the Sorites paradox, the following must be true: For any of its disjuncts, any accurate and univocal interpretation of the disjunction will not make the disjunct counterintuitive, assuming it makes the disjunct true. Let's examine each disjunct in turn to see how the objection fares.

The Semantic Complexity objection applied to SD_1 says that any accurate and univocal interpretation of the disjunction that makes SD_1 come out true won't make it counterintuitive. If SD_1 is true, so "It's not the case that anyone with less than \$1 is poor" is true under some accurate interpretation, it is either true or not true in ordinary discourse. If it is true in ordinary discourse – in *any* actual contexts that preserve its basic meaning (so, e.g., we don't give it a *new* meaning, such as an acceptable precisification of "financially poor") – that fact is wildly counterintuitive, on straightforward empirical grounds. I don't see how contextual issues could change that result. On the other hand, if it is never, in any actual contexts, true in ordinary discourse but is true under some other accurate interpretation, then we have been wildly wrong about interpretation. Both options are philosophically counterintuitive. So, the objection fails for SD_1.

Virtually the same reasoning applies to SD_2 and SD_3. So the objection won't work for them either. SD_4 and SD_5 need separate treatment.

The Semantic Complexity objection applied to SD_4 says that any accurate and univocal interpretation of the disjunction that makes SD_4 come out true won't make it counterintuitive. The objection needs to be applied to both ways SD_4 can be true, given in the previous section. Regarding the first way (viz. the simple sentential inference rule in question isn't truth-preserving when applied to pairs of very simple sentences), SD_4 says "(1) and (2) are true, (3) isn't true, and the first disjunct of (1) is indeed the negation of (2)." I can't think of a way to accurately interpret that claim so that it's both true and not counterintuitive.

Regarding the second way (viz. the sentential inference rule is truth-preserving but doesn't apply to the SCs, because the middle SCs aren't disjunctions), SD_4 says that the middle SCs aren't disjunctions. But look, we are the ones who articulated the middle SCs. In order for the second way to hold, it has to be the case that despite our intentions we simply have failed to make the middle SCs disjunctions – and, the crucial point, this fact isn't philosophically counterintuitive. That's clearly false: It certainly is counterintuitive to think the middle SCs aren't disjunctions! Again, I'm not saying that the middle SCs are disjunctions. I'm okay with them being something else. All I'm saying is that it's philosophically counterintuitive. So, the objection fails for SD_4.

The Semantic Complexity objection applied to SD_5 says that any accurate and univocal interpretation of the disjunction that makes SD_5 come out true won't make it counterintuitive. SD_5 says that both "Anyone with less than $\$10^{12}$ is poor" and "It's not the case that anyone with less than $\$10^{12}$ is rich" are true. Hence, if the objection works for SD_5, it's not counterintuitive that there are true contradictions built up from ordinary, non-liar-type sentences, and it's not counterintuitive that "It is not the case that anyone with less than $\$10^{12}$ is rich" is true. Both claims are obviously false. So, the objection fails for SD_5.

Hence, there is excellent reason to think the Semantic Complexity objection fails when applied to the Sorites paradox.

For my third and final comment on the Semantic Complexity Objection, assume for the sake of argument that I'm wrong about *all* of the foregoing. So, contrary to what I just argued/stated, the following is true: For any disjunct SD, any accurate and univocal interpretation of the disjunction that makes SD true fails to make it philosophically counterintuitive. So both parts (a) and (b) of the Semantic Complexity objection are true. But, as I will now prove, that consequence is *itself* a philosophically counterintuitive result! In that sense, if the objector is right, then I still win: There is a philosophically counterintuitive conclusion to the Sorites. Let me explain this odd result.

Suppose the Semantic Complexity objection is right. That entails that all the following claims are true:

Any accurate interpretation of SD_1 that makes it true fails to make it counterintuitive.

Any accurate interpretation of SD_2 that makes it true fails to make it counterintuitive.

Any accurate interpretation of SD_3 that makes it true fails to make it counterintuitive.

Any accurate interpretation of SD_4 that makes it true fails to make it counterintuitive.

Any accurate interpretation of SD_5 that makes it true fails to make it counterintuitive.

But if all (or really any) of those claims is true, then we have been wildly wrong about the interpretation of the SDs. And that fact fits the definition of "philosophically counterintuitive." Hence, even if the objection succeeds so each true disjunct is not "directly" philosophically counterintuitive, it's still the case that the true SD disjunct is "indirectly" philosophically counterintuitive via the truth of the corresponding indented claim above. Therefore, we have proven that the Semantic Complexity objection is powerless to avoid the result that the truth of the Sorites CD requires a philosophically counterintuitive result.

As an aside, I think the Semantic Complexity objection fails for the Skepticism paradox as well, despite the superficial aptness of using the latter to illustrate the former. Suppose the Semantic Complexity objection is true applied to skepticism. That means the following is true:

> Under any accurate interpretation that makes "Jo is in a position to know that she's not a mere brain in a vat" true, it is not philosophically counterintuitive; and under any accurate interpretation that makes "Jo doesn't know she has two woolly mammoths" true, it is not philosophically counterintuitive.

But that indented claim is philosophically counterintuitive, which means both E_2 and E_3 are indirectly counterintuitive. If the straightforward version of Attributor Contextualism is the solution to the Skeptical problem – and not merely true – that's a surprising result – a counterintuitive one.

7 A Doxastically Distressing Disjunction: The Liar

The method of analysis used for the Sorites can be applied to some other philosophical problems in such a way as to generate other doxastically distressing disjunctions that have philosophically counterintuitive disjuncts. Here are twenty such problems as candidates (they are mere candidates; I do not claim that each *in fact* generates a doxastically distressing disjunction that has philosophically counterintuitive disjuncts):

> The Statue–Clay problem, Curry's paradox, the Grelling–Nelson paradox, the No–No paradox, the Paradox of the Knower, Fitch's paradox, the Surprise Exam, the Ship of Theseus, the St. Petersburg paradox, the Suspense paradox, Russell's paradox, Yablo's paradox, the Dogmatism paradox, the Liar paradox, the Problem of the Many (see Section 8), the Tibbles–Tib problem, the Preface paradox, the argument for skepticism, the relativity of simultaneity paradox, and van Inwagen's argument for incompatibilism.

Extending the list is a matter of patience and familiarity with the many fields of philosophy.

The problems need not even be labeled "paradox." What is needed to prove a surprising and doxastically distressing disjunction is this: A philosophy problem that generates (1) a set of individually highly intuitive claims such that, when subject to (2) highly intuitively truth-preserving inference rules, (3) can apparently be used to derive the negation of a highly intuitive claim (it need not be a contradiction).

In order to see further applications of my method of problem analysis, let's look at one of the other classic philosophical problems: the Liar paradox. We can use the following five C claims in order to generate the paradox, with "Alf" a name of a paradoxical sentence type (with appropriate adjustments, we could focus on sentence tokens or propositions instead).

LC_1: Alf = "Alf isn't true." (It certainly seems as though we could use a proper name stipulation to make C_1 true. Alternatively, we could instead fix the referent of "Alf" via a definite description such as "The third indented sentence type on page 774.")

LC_2: If Alf = "Alf isn't true" and Alf is true, then "Alf isn't true" is true. (Cf. if D = "Dogs bark" and D is true, then "Dogs bark" is true.)[2]

LC_3: If Alf = "Alf isn't true" and "Alf isn't true" is true, then Alf is true. (Cf. if D = "Dogs bark" and "Dogs bark" is true, then D is true.)

LC_4: If "Alf isn't true" is true, then Alf isn't true. (Cf. if "Dogs bark" is true, then dogs bark.)

LC_5: If Alf isn't true, then "Alf isn't true" is true. (Cf. if dogs bark, then "Dogs bark" is true.)

If you tinker with them for a bit, you can see how to derive $\sim LC_1$ from LC_2–LC_5, which, if truth-preserving, would of course make the LCs jointly inconsistent ("LC" = liar claim). As with the Sorites, this Element is not concerned with the solutions to the Liar paradox. I don't care what your favored solution is, I don't want to listen to you blather on about it, and it won't matter to my arguments at all.

Consider the following claims, which reference the liar LCs ("LD" for "liar disjunct," analogous to "SD" for "sorites disjunct"):

LD_1: $\sim LC_1$

LD_2: $\sim LC_2$

LD_3: $\sim LC_3$

LD_4: $\sim LC_4$

LD_5: $\sim LC_5$

LD_6: LC_1 & LC_2 & LC_3 & LC_4 & LC_5 & there is no truth-preserving derivation to a contradiction

LD7: LC_1 & LC_2 & LC_3 & LC_4 & LC_5 & there is a truth-preserving derivation to a contradiction

---

[2] LC_2 and LC_3 are instances of the general principles known as Release and Capture. We do not need the general principles in order to generate the paradox.

The reader can verify with mere sentential logic that the disjunction of the seven Ls is logically true. Thus, the disjunction of the seven LDs is true; that is the Disjunctive Analysis (DA) disjunction for the Liar. So far, the argument is indisputable as long as one isn't going to reject the truth-preserving nature of the simplest rules of sentential logic.

Let's examine the philosophical consequences of the disjuncts of the DA. As with the Sorites, my brief commentaries are meant to prove a Consequence disjunction for the Liar, each disjunct of which is philosophically counterintuitive. I am not arguing that any particular disjunct is not true (or is true).

LD_1:   It's not the case that Alf = "Alf isn't true."

LD_1's being true would mean that we can't set up "Alf" so that it refers to "Alf isn't true." Almost everyone in the philosophy of language agrees that we can stipulate that we will use "Alf" as a name for "Alf isn't true"; if LD_1 is right, all these philosophers are wrong. Further, almost everyone would agree that we can use a reference-fixing description such as "The third indented sentence type on page 774" in order to refer to Alf; if LD_1 is true, this is mistaken as well. I'm *not* saying that those philosophers are correct. I don't care if they are and I don't care if they aren't. All I'm pointing out is that LD_1's truth would overthrow an enormous part of what is taken for granted in the philosophy of language regarding the basics of reference. Hence, we have proven that LD_1 is philosophically counterintuitive.

Just like with the Sorites, there is another possibility – but this time it's not clear that it even makes sense. Suppose LD_1 is true, so "Alf = 'Alf isn't true'" isn't true as that sentence is used in this work of philosophy. But perhaps that sentence is true when used in ordinary discourse; so the relevant bridge premise is false. And if it is true in ordinary discourse, then its being false in philosophical discourse may not be nearly as counterintuitive; in addition, it won't follow, at least immediately, that a great many of our ordinary commonsensical beliefs, or a significant portion of our most confidently held beliefs or belief-dispositions, are not true.

But does that make sense? The sentence "Alf = 'Alf isn't true'" would be an odd addition to "ordinary discourse." It's difficult to even imagine how the sentence could end up with different truth-values in the two discourses. Furthermore, the highly counterintuitive nature of the sentence's being false comes from philosophy, not ordinary discourse; there is little reason to care what our attitudes would be towards that sentence outside a philosophical context. Moreover, just like with the sorites, there is no basis for positing the alethic difference.

LD_2: It's not the case that: if Alf = "Alf isn't true" and Alf is true, then "Alf isn't true" is true.

If LD_2 is true, then since LC_2 is a material conditional by design, Alf = "Alf isn't true," Alf is true, and yet "Alf isn't true" isn't true. That looks remarkably like a logical falsehood. Most of us think that logical falsehoods aren't true. Hence, LD_2 is philosophically counterintuitive.

LD_3: It's not the case that: if Alf = "Alf isn't true" and "Alf isn't true" is true, then Alf is true.

If LD_3 is true, then since LC_3 is a material conditional by design, Alf = "Alf isn't true," "Alf isn't true" is true, and yet Alf isn't true. This is just like LD_2: an apparent logical falsehood.

LD_4: It's not the case that: if "Alf isn't true" is true, then Alf isn't true.

If LD_4 is true, then since LC_4 is a material conditional by design, "Alf isn't true" is true and yet Alf is true. That might not be a logical falsehood, but it is philosophically counterintuitive.

LD_5: It's not the case that: if Alf isn't true, then "Alf isn't true" is true.

If LD_5 is true, then since LC_5 is a material conditional by design, Alf isn't true and yet "Alf isn't true" isn't true. As with LD_4, that might not be a logical falsehood but it is philosophically counterintuitive.

LD_6: LC_1 & LC_2 & LC_3 & LC_4 & LC_5 & there is no truth-preserving derivation to a contradiction.

If you gaze at LC_1–LC_5, you'll see how to infer ~LC_1 from them using just elementary inferences from sentential logic (provisionally assume LC_1 and then derive a contradiction). It is very difficult for most of us to see how any of those inferences fails to be truth-preserving, which is what the truth of LD_6 requires.

To say this is *not* to assume or imply that first-order logic can "fully capture" the logical form of each of LC_1–LC_5, whatever "fully capture" means here. *Even if FOL cannot "capture" at least one of the LCs, it would be philosophically significant to learn that one of the inference rules applied to the LCs isn't truth-preserving.* The significance would come from the disjunctive consequences of LD_6: Either the elementary inference-types are truth-preserving but we have badly misunderstood the meanings of the LC sentences (so the rules are fine but mysteriously don't apply to at least one of the LCs) or we have understood the meanings of the LC sentences but the inference-types aren't truth-preserving (the meanings are fine but the rules aren't). (Or *both* the rules and meanings aren't fine.) Hence, the truth of LD_6 would have profound implications for either (a) how we understand linguistic meaning, since the LCs are quite simple sentences but we don't understand them, or (b) how we understand logic, since the inferences are quite simple and seemingly truth-preserving. Hence, LD_6 is philosophically counterintuitive.

LD_7: LC_1 & LC_2 & LC_3 & LC_4 & LC_5 & there is a truth-preserving derivation to a contradiction.

If LD_7 is true, then two things follow immediately. First, $\sim LC_1$ is true, which is philosophically counterintuitive for the reasons given for LD_1. Second, LD_7 is obviously contradictory, which is philosophically counterintuitive as well.

It is worth remembering that paradoxical Liar sentences need not be bizarre like "This sentence isn't true." For instance, it's well known that sentences such as "What Jo said about Trump just isn't true" can generate Liar paradoxes too. Hence, if we accept LD_7 then we will have to accept *loads* of contradictions (even if we adopt a paraconsistent logic, so that it's not the case that everything follows from just one contradiction). So, if LD_7 is true, then we have true contradictions galore.

In the preceding brief commentary on the LDs, I am *not* arguing that any one of them is false. There's no argument here for or against dialethism, the Revenge or Capture parts of the T-schema, or anything else along those lines. So, if you accept or reject one of those views, stop complaining. In fact, you should be celebrating: I'm only arguing that each disjunct is philosophically counterintuitive.

We have proven that at least one of the following is true – and that each bullet point satisfies the definition of "philosophically counterintuitive":

- We can neither stipulate that "Alf" will refer to "Alf isn't true" nor use a definite description such as "The third indented sentence on page 774" to set up the reference for "Alf." (LD_1 and first disjunctive consequence of LD_7.)
- Some apparent elementary logical falsehoods are true. (LD_2 and LD_3.)
- Alf isn't true but "Alf isn't true" isn't true; or "Alf isn't true" is true but it's not the case that Alf isn't true. (LD_4 and LD_5.)
- Simple inference rules aren't truth-preserving when applied to relatively simple sentences; or we have little idea how to interpret a significant portion of our simple sentences. (LD_6.)

- There are a great many true contradictions, even assuming a paraconsistent logic. (Second disjunctive consequence of LD_7.)

Naturally, some philosophers who have thought long and hard about these paradoxes have grown quite comfortable with the particular solution they endorse. After enough time, the solution might not even seem counterintuitive to them; such is the life of an intellectual person spending years dealing with hard philosophical problems ending up in a certain peculiar kind of communal doxastic bubble. But we should not confuse "That solution should not be counterintuitive" with "That solution is not philosophically counterintuitive." I have been arguing against the latter, not the former. The significance of philosophical counterintuitiveness is discussed in Section 12.

8 A Doxastically Distressing Disjunction: The Problem of the Many

Another classic problem is the Problem of the Many, which can be captured with these six claims ("P" for "Problem," "C" for "claim"):

PC_1: There is at least one tree in my backyard.

PC_2: Every tree in my backyard is exhaustively (not partially) composed of chemical atoms.

PC_3: For every tree in my backyard that is composed of chemical atoms (at a time), there is a group of chemical (not mereological) atoms that composes it (at that time). (Some would say, with reason, that there is exactly one such group; PC_3 is more cautious.)

PC_4: For every group of chemical atoms that composes a tree in my backyard, there is a group of chemical atoms with at least some distinct chemical atoms that composes a tree in my backyard. (The large groups – e.g. about 10^{30} chemical atoms in each – in question are literally about 99.99999999999999999999999999 percent overlapping and are, to all appearances, equally good candidates for composing a tree.)

PC_5: No tree in my backyard is exhaustively composed of distinctly membered (in chemical atoms) groups of chemical atoms.

PC_6: There is at most one tree in my backyard.

This time one needs predicate logic to derive $\sim PC_6$ from PC_1–PC_5; it's not the case that every exhaustive analysis of a sharp philosophical problem will require mere sentential logic to derive a contradiction. Here are the relevant claims for exhaustively analyzing the Problem of the Many, again using the method illustrated twice before ("P" for "Problem," "D" for "disjunct").

PD_1: $\sim PC_1$

PD_2: $\sim PC_2$

PD_3: $\sim PC_3$

PD_4: $\sim PC_4$

PD_5: $\sim PC_5$

PD_6: $\sim PC_6$

PD_7: PC_1 & PC_2 & PC_3 & PC_4 & PC_5 & PC_6 & there is no truth-preserving derivation to a contradiction

PD_8: PC_1 & PC_2 & PC_3 & PC_4 & PC_5 & PC_6 & there is a truth-preserving derivation to a contradiction

The reader can verify with sentential logic that the disjunction of the eight PDs is true. As before, let's examine the obvious, immediate philosophical consequences of each disjunct, PD_1–PD_8, in order.

PD_1:   It's not the case that there is at least one tree in my backyard.

If PD_1 is true in this Element, then it is either true or not true in ordinary discourse. If it is true in ordinary discourse, that is wildly counterintuitive, on straightforward empirical grounds. If it is not true in ordinary discourse (but true in this Element), then we have been wildly wrong about interpretation. Both options are philosophically counterintuitive: They are inconsistent with either a great many of our ordinary commonsensical beliefs, a significant portion of our most confidently held ordinary beliefs or belief-dispositions, or key philosophical ideas held by many contemporary philosophers. Hence, PD_1 itself is philosophically counterintuitive, either directly (if it's true in ordinary discourse) or indirectly (if it's true in this Element but false in ordinary discourse, despite my linguistic instructions; see discussion of bridge premises in Section 4).

PD_2:   It's not the case that every tree in my backyard is composed of chemical atoms.

If PD_2 is true in this Element, then it's true in ordinary discourse. If it's true in ordinary discourse, then we have a philosophically counterintuitive result, as any scientifically informed person could tell you. And if it's not true in ordinary discourse, because the relevant bridge premise is false, we still have a philosophically counterintuitive result for the same reason we had one in the case of PD_1.

PD_3:   It's not the case that for every tree in my backyard that is composed of chemical atoms, there is a group of chemical atoms that composes it.

If PD_3 is true in this Element, then a tree in my backyard is composed of atom A1, atom A2, atom A3, . . . (and the list is not infinite). But there is no group of atoms that composes it. If so, that is philosophically counterintuitive, as it goes firmly against key philosophical ideas held by many philosophers, if not natural scientists. (We didn't need a bridge premise here.)

PD_4:   It's not the case that for every group of chemical atoms that composes a tree in my backyard, there is a group of chemical atoms with at least some distinct chemical atoms that composes a tree in my backyard.

I already discussed PD_4 indirectly with the Sorites, so some of what I say here is repetition.

If PD_4 is true in this Element, then there is a group of chemical atoms, G, that composes a tree in my backyard – call that tree T_G – but there is no distinctly membered group of atoms that composes a tree in my backyard (either T_G or any other tree). Clearly, G has got to have something like 10^{30} chemical atoms (give or take a few orders of magnitude) in order to compose a tree in my backyard, as atoms are very small compared to ordinary trees in backyards. So, now take groups G_1–$G_{million}$, each of which contains the atoms in G plus or minus exactly one borderline case chemical atom. Given the way ordinary trees are, with enormous numbers of borderline cases of atoms, it's clear that these million Gs exist provided G exists. If PD_4 is true, then none of G_1-$G_{million}$ compose a tree in my backyard. Hence, *there are more than a million perfectly ordinary treeish groups of atoms that are literally 99.99999999999999999999999999 percent overlapping but only one of which composes a tree in my backyard.*

PD_4 is not saying that those other Gs fail to compose T_G specifically. Instead, it's saying that those other Gs fail to compose any tree at all (clearly, if they don't compose a tree in my backyard, they don't compose one elsewhere). Either those other Gs don't compose anything at all – but how is G so magical compared to them that it composes something while they don't? – or they do compose things but those things aren't trees – but how could those things not be trees if the thing composed by virtually identical G is a tree? This means that a perfectly ordinary use of "tree in my backyard" is stupefyingly, staggeringly precise, favoring G over G_1–$G_{million}$ despite their virtual identity. But how on earth did "is a tree in my backyard" *acquire* such an amazingly discriminating meaning? No one has offered even the faintest plausible story, and there is good reason to think none is forthcoming.

With some work, one could offer a *stipulation* regarding "is a tree in my backyard" so that under the resulting interpretation PD_4 is true and not philosophically counterintuitive. This would be similar to choosing a sharp cutoff for "is poor," as in the Sorites. However, that fact doesn't suggest for an instant that the sentence *already,* in the actual world prior to our possible stipulation, has an accurate interpretation with that consequence.

If you accept PD_4, then you surely have to wonder what shocking falsehoods there are about language and thought that you have hitherto presumed in all your work. Perhaps you have grown comfortable with accepting many other comparably outrageous epistemicist ideas, such as the idea that a perfectly ordinary token of "The restaurant is a short walk from here" goes from true to not true in the space of a yoctometer (10^{-24} m). It's great that you have managed to accept linguistic miracles; it's impressive that you have gotten over your *previous* discomfort with some radical claims. But then why think your *continuing* discomfort with any other radical claim isn't misguided as well? I won't repeat the arguments from the Sorites paradox.

PD_5: It's not the case that no tree in my backyard is composed of distinctly membered (in chemical atoms) groups of chemical atoms.

If PD_5 is true in this Element, then there are at least two distinctly membered groups of atoms that both compose (at a time) the very same tree in my backyard. Since the groups differ in atom membership, there is chemical atom in one but not the other; call such an atom A. Hence, it appears that at a particular moment the tree is partially composed of A and not partially composed of A. Unless we have made a truly fundamental error in how to think of composition at a time, we have a contradiction (millions of them, for other Problem of the Many cases). Of course, I am *not* saying that we have made no such fundamental error. All I am saying is that the results – either true contradictions or the fundamental error – are philosophically counterintuitive since they go against key philosophical ideas held by many contemporary philosophers.

PD_6: It's not the case that there is at most one tree in my backyard.

If PD_6 is true in this Element, then there are at least two trees in my backyard – despite the fact that any non-philosopher or botanist would swear on their life that there's just one tree there. I omit the standard comments on the relevant bridge premise.

PD_7: PC_1 & PC_2 & PC_3 & PC_4 & PC_5 & PC_6 & there is no truth-preserving derivation to a contradiction.

If you gaze at PC_1–PC_5, you'll be able to work out how to infer $\sim PC_6$ from them using just four elementary inferences. If PD_7 is true, then at least one of the four is not truth-preserving (or the inference from P and Q to (P & Q) isn't truth-preserving). Here are the four inferences in question:

I1: From both

  PC_1: There is at least one tree in my backyard
  PC_2: Every tree in my backyard is composed of chemical atoms

To

There is at least one tree in my backyard that is composed of chemical atoms.

I2: From both

There is at least one tree in my backyard that is composed of chemical atoms

  PC_3: For every tree in my backyard that is composed of chemical atoms, there is a group of chemical atoms that composes it

To

There is at least one group of chemical atoms that composes a tree in my backyard.

I3: From both

There is at least one group of chemical atoms that composes a tree in my backyard

  PC_4: For every group of chemical atoms that composes a tree in my backyard, there is a group of chemical atoms with at least some distinct chemical atoms that composes a tree in my backyard

To

There are groups of chemical atoms that are distinctly membered (in chemical atoms) and that both compose trees in my backyard.

I4: From both

There are groups of chemical atoms that are distinctly membered (in chemical atoms) and that both compose trees in my backyard

  PC_5: No tree in my backyard is composed of distinctly membered (in chemical atoms) groups of chemical atoms

To

  $\sim PC_6$: It is not the case that there is at most one tree in my backyard.

It is very difficult to see how any of these four inferences fails to be truth-preserving, which is what the truth of PD_7 requires. As with the Sorites, to say this is *not* to assume or imply that first-order logic can "capture" the logical form of each of PC_1–PC_6, whatever "capture" means here. The significance of P_7 comes from its disjunctive consequences: Either the four inference-types are truth-preserving but we have badly misunderstood the meanings of the PC sentences (so the four rules are fine but don't apply to at least one of the PCs) or we have understood the meanings of the PC sentences but at least one of the inference-types isn't truth-preserving (the meanings are fine but the rules aren't). (Or *both* the rules and meanings aren't fine.) Hence, the truth of PD_7 would have profound implications for either (a) how we understand linguistic meaning, since the PCs are quite simple sentences but we don't understand them, or (b) how we understand logic, since the inferences are quite simple and seemingly truth-preserving. And recall the point made earlier in this section: There is an enormous number and variety of instances of the Problem of the Many, so (a) and (b) go far beyond the six PCs. Hence, PD_7 is philosophically counterintuitive.

PD_8: PC_1 & PC_2 & PC_3 & PC_4 & PC_5 & PC_6 & there is a truth-preserving derivation to a contradiction.

If PD_8 is true, then two things follow. First, $\sim PC_6$ is true (because PD_8 says the obvious derivation to the contradiction (PC_6 & $\sim PC_6$) goes through), which is philosophically counterintuitive for the reasons given for PD_6. Second, PC_6 is both true and not true, which is philosophically counterintuitive as well – especially since none of the PCs is even a paradoxical sentence, such as those from the Liar and other semantic paradoxes.

Since there is an enormous variety and number of cases that fit the Problem of the Many template, if we think the one I've used above regarding the tree in my backyard reveals a pair of true contradictory claims, then an enormous variety and number of other pairs of contradictory claims are true too (even if we adopt a paraconsistent logic, so that it's not the case that everything follows from just the contradiction in the backyard tree case).

My arguments regarding the obvious, immediate philosophical consequences of the individual PD disjuncts, plus the logically true premise that at least one PD disjunct is true, prove that at least one of the following is both true and philosophically counterintuitive:

- "There are no trees" is true in ordinary discourse. (First disjunctive consequence of PD_1; the other disjunctive consequence, from the bridge premise, is
  covered in the last bullet point.)

- "Trees aren't composed of chemical atoms" is true in ordinary discourse. (First disjunctive consequence of PD_2; the other disjunctive consequence, from the bridge premise, is covered in the last bullet point.)
- Trees are composed of chemical atoms but for a given tree there's no group of chemical atoms that composes it. (PD_3.)
- "Tree in my backyard" (as well as an enormous number of similar phrases) is amazingly precise in the sense that there are there are more than a million perfectly ordinary treeish groups of chemical atoms in my backyard that are *literally* 99.99999999999999999999999999 percent overlapping but only one thing satisfies "tree in my backyard." (PD_4.)
- At any given time, a tree is composed of multiple groups of chemical atoms that differ in atom membership (so the tree is composed of a group of chemical atoms that includes atom X but the tree is also, simultaneously, composed of a group of chemical atoms that fails to include X). (PD_5.)
- "There are at least two trees in my backyard" is true in ordinary discourse despite the fact that any non-philosopher or botanist would swear on their life that there's just one tree there. (First disjunctive consequence of PD_6 and PD_8; the other disjunctive consequence of PD_6 is covered in the last bullet point.)
- Some of the simplest and most certain inference rules aren't truth-preserving when applied to relatively simple, non-paradoxical sentences, so we have been wildly wrong about elementary logic; or we have little idea how to interpret an enormous number and variety of our ordinary, everyday, simple, non-paradoxical sentences. (PD_7.)
- There are a great many true contradictions coming from ordinary sentences (not weird, liar-type ones), even assuming a paraconsistent logic. (Second disjunctive consequence of PD_8.)
- PD_1, PD_2, and PD_6 are true in this Element but false in ordinary discourse, despite not containing philosophical jargon and contrary to my author instructions. (Second disjunctive consequence of PD_1, PD_2, and PD_6.)

We could subject more philosophical problems to the method of analysis I have illustrated three times now – although it's worth keeping in mind the possibility that the Semantic Complexity Objection will diminish the significance of some of those problems.

9 Knockdown Arguments and Philosophical Agreement

It often seems as though philosophers can't agree on anything philosophically significant. Even so, I think there are a great many substantive philosophical claims that we almost unanimously agree on. Since I have dealt with this issue elsewhere (Frances 2017), I won't go into the details.

What would be really interesting – and similar to what we find in the sciences – is agreement on *philosophically significant* claims. Just think of potential examples: agreement regarding epistemic externalism, Platonism for abstract objects, type identity theory, act-utilitarianism, Kripke's causal-historical theory of proper name reference transmission, and so on. It may seem that such agreement is virtually nonexistent.

On a related matter, it may seem naïve to think that there are any knock-down arguments in philosophy for philosophically substantive theses. If there were, then presumably we would have agreement on their conclusions – which shows the connection between my two topics of agreement and knock-down argument. Perhaps we can give knockdown arguments for platitudes, and formal logic and other formal sciences can produce knockdown arguments for formal theses, but it doesn't seem like there are any knockdown arguments for truly philosophically significant nonformal claims – virtually however one wants to precisify "philosophically significant" so that it comes out interesting.

Contrary to those views, I think we can, via knockdown arguments that belong firmly to philosophy, find agreement on substantive matters in philosophy – which give us philosophical progress. The doxastically distressing CDs do the trick.

Here, finally, are my book's first four (of ten) theses, which touch on these topics of knockdown philosophical arguments, and philosophical agreement:

T_1: The CDs for the Sorites, Liar, and Problem of the Many are true.

T_2: Each disjunct of those CDs is philosophically counterintuitive.

T_3: The arguments for T_1 and T_2 are knockdown arguments in at least most of the senses of "knockdown argument" used in common accusations such as "Unlike the sciences, philosophy has no knockdown arguments."

T_4: We agree that the CDs are true and their disjuncts are philosophically counterintuitive.

My arguments regarding the *obvious, immediate* consequences of each of the components of the three sample paradoxes, with the conclusions of those arguments summarized in the CDs, are clearly sound, as those arguments were so unambitious. So, T_1 is true. Moreover, it does not take much experience in philosophy or ordinary life to know that each disjunct is philosophically counterintuitive (this feature of the disjuncts is a sociological fact, not a normative one). Hence, T_2 is true too.

One might object to T_2 on the grounds that disputes about the CD disjuncts are "merely verbal" and thus not really counterintuitive. However, the arguments for the counterintuitiveness of the CD disjuncts addressed questions of interpretation, so objections about the prevalence of context dependence and other linguistic shenanigans are useless here. In addition, the use of "merely" is crucial. Even if disputes about the CD disjuncts (all of them? seriously?) are "verbal," that does not, at all, mean they are "merely verbal." Even if the disputes about each of the CD disjuncts were really about language in some deep sense, there isn't the slightest reason to think they all have the import of disputing "Does that ridiculous drink count as a martini?" (see Bennett 2009). Linguistic issues can be philosophically significant.

In addition, thesis T_6 (articulated and defended in Section 10) entails that there are a great many disjuncts, from CDs generated from other philosophical problems. It's hardly plausible that the disputes about *every* disjunct from *every* paradoxical CD are merely verbal.

Regarding T_2 again, we are familiar with claims turning out true even though we quite reasonably were extremely confident they were false. Lottery claims such as "My neighbor won the lottery" fit the bill. Such claims are highly improbable but not counterintuitive. Although the disjuncts of our doxastically distressing CDs are similar to lottery claims in being highly improbable, they are crucially different as well for the following reasons.

First, you knew that there would be a lottery winner. But you didn't know that one of the disjuncts had to be true. The lottery disjunction "Ticket 1 won, or ticket 2 won, or ..." was already known to be true, or at least very probable; but the philosophical disjunctions weren't like that at all. It's genuinely surprising to learn that those disjunctions are true; that's why we are amazed at those philosophical problems in the first place. Once one has a good grasp of the problem, one sees, at least dimly, that *any* solution to the problem will be deeply counterintuitive. A good portion of my argument thus far proves it.

Second, discovering that your neighbor won the lottery will not give you any reason to distrust your judgment about your neighbor, lotteries, or anything else. But learning that at least one of the CD disjuncts is true is completely different. If any of those disjuncts hold – and one of them *must*, as we saw in Section 5 – then we have been wildly wrong about language, logic, empirical matters, or truth. Lottery claims aren't anything like that.

That is all I have to say in defense of T_1 and T_2.

In order to get anywhere in addressing the question central to T_3, "Are there any knockdown arguments in nonformal philosophy?," it might be thought that we need to define the key term "knockdown argument." I don't think there is a set semantics for "knockdown argument" – even when embedded in the relevant claims such as "There are no knockdown arguments in philosophy, although there are some in science." At the least, it's a polysemous term with no philosophically central truth-conditional disambiguation. We could spend a fair amount of time debating various potential meanings. I will set aside the semantic issue because I hold that it's more interesting to ask, "How good do philosophical arguments get? And how does that compare with science for instance?" I think those are the relevant questions to ask because when it comes to the general topic of "knockdown arguments" in philosophy, there are two thoughts that are front and center: the worry that arguments in philosophy are always controversial even amongst the relevant experts, at least if the arguments have substantive conclusions; and the worry that since in the sciences there are plenty of uncontroversial arguments for substantive conclusions, philosophy's lack of them is a mark against it. We need not use "knockdown argument" in this discussion.

One insight that I think helps us in addressing those questions concerns the context-sensitivity of argument assessment.

For example, in a discussion in epistemology regarding what it takes for a belief to amount to knowledge, it wouldn't be fair to bring up eliminative materialism. In a discussion in philosophical aesthetics, it would be beside the point to address color eliminativism, which says that there are no colors in paintings, pictures, films, or other art works. In a debate in the philosophy of sport, it would be odd to require the debaters to address compositional nihilism, which says there is no sporting equipment. More interestingly, whereas in many philosophy of mind contexts it's appropriate to ignore eliminative materialism, in other philosophy of mind contexts it is not.

With these cases in mind, perhaps we could construct a notion of a knockdown argument so that an argument can be knockdown relative to some but not all "contexts" – and we would use the above examples as hints on how to fill out the latter notion, probably having something to do with presuppositions regarding argument evaluation (as a way of filling out the idea that some criticisms are "fair" but others are not). The notion of a knockdown argument "in philosophy" would have to be modified, as the eliminative materialism example suggests: A given argument can be knockdown in some but not all philosophical "contexts," so the question "Is this a knockdown – or completely uncontroversial – argument in philosophy?" does not always have a right answer. For instance, one can offer an argument for "Some people have very poor evidence for their true beliefs" that is knockdown relative to epistemological contexts (one could argue for it via detailed presentation of an actual example) but not relative to some contexts in metaphysics or other areas of philosophy (in which the existence of beliefs or truths are at issue).

Some people will say that "Some people have very poor evidence for their true beliefs" isn't a philosophically substantive conclusion. But that's just false for at least some entirely reasonable precisifications of "philosophically substantive." For one thing, the conclusion in question is controversial *amongst philosophers* relative to discussions for which radical views such as eliminative materialism or the inconsistency view of truth are relevant. For another thing, any philosopher who listens carefully to non-philosophers, such as college students, knows that the conclusion is controversial for non-philosophers (which of course is not to say that all or even most non-philosophers go so far as to disagree with it). Even if the conclusion were not controversial amongst philosophers, that would hardly mean it isn't philosophically substantive. "Heavy objects fall just as fast as light ones, other things equal" is scientifically substantive even though it's not controversial amongst scientifically educated people.

The Holy Grail of knockdown arguments would be an argument that is knockdown with respect to *every* context – or perhaps virtually every context. These would be arguments that would be nearly universally accepted as sound by the relevant experts who were thoroughly familiar with the arguments. I suspect that when philosophers say "There are no knockdown arguments in philosophy," what they mean, charitably put, is that there are no such Holy Grail arguments. Are there any? A personal story might help.

Years ago, I thought that one of the strongest arguments in all of philosophy was this, with respect to the sorites:

- $\{SC_1\text{-}SC_{LAST}\}$ is inconsistent
- SC_1 is true
- SC_{LAST} is true
- Hence, for at least one of the middle SCs, it's not the case that it is true

That is argument (1). It's the basic argument for epistemicism, and it just seemed crashingly obvious that it was deductively valid and had three true premises. It's extraordinary how philosophers who don't work on vagueness will spend large amounts of time huffing and puffing about borderline cases, semantic indeterminacy, and loads of other considerations but never bother to do the real work: *take a stand on the three-premise argument immediately above*. All that clever talk is pure evasion. I thought to myself, "Honestly, is there a better argument in all of philosophy? Maybe the Liar argument for a contradiction, but that's about it."

Then I thought, well, that's too quick. Maybe (1) is mistaken. All we can be really sure of is the first premise: $\{SC_1\text{-}SC_{LAST}\}$ is inconsistent. We can prove that with logic alone; call that *argument (2)*. Maybe SC_1, "Anyone worth less than \$1 (US) is (financially) poor," is false but, for some "technical" reason, its being false doesn't ruin its status as perfectly fine to rely upon in any ordinary or scientific context. Or perhaps that was true of SC_{LAST}. In any case, we can start with (2)'s soundness.

Then I thought we can't be certain (2) is sound either. Perhaps some contradictions are true, as some logicians insist. Paraconsistent logics might complicate things too; since I was no philosopher of logic, I didn't know my way around that issue at all. Or maybe some elementary inference rule isn't truth-preserving, as some logicians insist. Sure, those options are highly counterintuitive, when well understood, but so is the negation of any of the SCs. I came to think that the logical argument (3) for the disjunctive conclusion "Either one of the SCs isn't true, a contradiction is true, or one of the relevant inference rules isn't truth-preserving" is a knockdown argument. We can start there, or so I thought.

But then I started worrying that there might be some semantic hocus-pocus present that ruins the derivation to a contradiction from the SCs. Perhaps all the SCs are true, contradictions aren't true, and the elementary inference rules in question (the ones that take us from the SCs to a contradiction) are truth-preserving; instead, the fault lies in our assumption that the inference rules *apply* to the SCs in the first place. Maybe the SCs are semantically complicated in some way that precludes the application of the sound inference rules. Lord knows that semantics has turned out to be complicated in surprising ways. There still is a knockdown argument in the vicinity, (4), but it is for the longer disjunction "Either one of the SCs isn't true, a contradiction is true, one of the relevant inference rules isn't truth-preserving, or the rules don't all apply to the SCs as we thought they did."

When one makes argument (4) precise, one gets the argument for the CD for the Sorites paradox. If you choose a reasonable and interesting characterization for "knockdown argument," so that there are such things in ordinary life or science and they are of *very* high strength, then I submit that the arguments for the CDs qualify. The arguments for "Each CD disjunct is philosophically counterintuitive" will as well. My reasons:

I argued for the CD via this means: the five-member disjunction of the SDs is true (end of Section 3); if at least one of the SDs is true, then one of the seven CD disjuncts is true (all of Section 4); hence, the seven-member CD is true. How might one object to this argument?

A radical view is this: my argument that the five-member disjunction of the SDs is unsound. Most people would say that all one needs to prove that disjunction is a truth table, since the disjunction is a truth of sentential logic. But perhaps it was a mistake for me to assume, in arguing for that disjunction, that the elementary rules of inference that gave us the disjunction of the five SDs are truth-preserving. Or, maybe it was a mistake for me to assume that those rules apply to the sorites SDs as expected; perhaps the rules are truth-preserving but the SDs have a structure that prevents the rules to apply to them in order to derive the five-member disjunction. Or, again, perhaps one of the two assumptions just mentioned is mistaken in my Section 4 arguments for the seven disjuncts, arguments of the form "If such-and-such SD is true, then such-and-such consequence follows."

But if any of those criticisms are right, then *the seven-membered CD is true* via the truth of either its fourth or fifth bullet point:

- At least one of the simplest sentential inference rules isn't truth-preserving when applied to pairs of very simple sentences.
- At least some of the middle SCs aren't even disjunctions.

Hence, it is going to be extremely difficult to avoid accepting the CD, since it looks as though the only way to object to its proof involves accepting the disjunction. Hence, T_3 is true.

One might object to the significance (not truth) of T_3 by saying that when philosophers claim that there are no knockdown arguments in philosophy, what they mean, charitably put, is that there aren't any for *particular philosophical positions*, such as externalism for epistemic justification or type identity theory. And I have done nothing to put pressure on *that* position on knockdown arguments. So, even though my T_3 looks controversial, it really isn't, since it doesn't go against any thesis anyone has actually defended when investigating the question of knockdown arguments in philosophy. In response, I agree that that is what at least some philosophers have implicitly meant (although I also think that they would insist on the stronger claim). I also agree that my arguments for CDs put no pressure on that position, as far as I know.

However, that certainly doesn't mean that my knockdown arguments for the CDs are not philosophically significant! In fact, the CDs for the Liar, Sorites, and Problem of the Many, for three examples, are by my lights *more* philosophically significant than a great many standard positions in philosophy, since each of the disjuncts is much more counterintuitive and philosophically significant than epistemic externalism, type identity theory, the equal weight view of peer disagreement, act-utilitarianism, and so on – and there are just a few disjuncts for each CD. Learning that one of them is true, which is what happens when we see the proofs of the CDs, means learning that we have been *wildly wrong* about language, empirical matters, or truth *in a fundamental manner*. I realize that others may disagree (benighted fools), but in my judgment that result is more significant than learning that epistemic externalism is true (which is not to cast aspersions). But I recognize that arguing with "Result X is more philosophically significant than result Y" is going to be pretty difficult and potentially unrewarding.

Sometimes philosophers go to great lengths to shift the goal posts when addressing the skeptic. We don't, these philosophers say, need to *convince* the skeptic she is wrong. Instead, we just have to convince neutral parties to the debate (All of them? Most? Should we do a poll every few years?). Perhaps there is a notion of a "knockdown argument" for X that need not actually convince any X-deniers.

On the face of it, this is silly: How good do you think your arguments for X are if you can't convince any of the advocates of ~X that you are right? It would be one thing if the group of advocates in question were morons, or brainwashed, or otherwise intellectually bereft. Needless to say (I hope), philosophers who are skeptics aren't like that. For another thing, I have long been one of those neutral parties even though I've read the arguments against skepticism but remain neutral.

In any case, I want the bar for a "knockdown argument" to be very high. I think that, for most any high bar, the arguments for the CDs meet it. That is the meaning behind T_3.

Let us move on to thesis T_4: the claim that *we agree* that the CDs are true and their disjuncts are philosophically counterintuitive. Interpreted as a descriptive claim, T_4 is obviously false, since almost no one has even thought about the CDs (so they can hardly be said to agree with them). After all, I just came up with them for this Element. So, I'm a liar and guilty of a bait-and-switch. I can retreat to a revised thesis:

T_4*:   We philosophers are *strongly disposed to* agree that the CDs are true and
             their disjuncts are philosophically counterintuitive – once we have
             thoroughly understood them.

That's much more plausible. Of course, philosophy being what it is, it's highly probable that at least some competent philosophers will object to my arguments for the CDs even after thinking about them carefully enough to understand them (a tall order). For instance, some of the doxastically stingy philosophers I mentioned when discussing knockdown arguments. But what percentage will? If it's low, as I expect, then T_4^* is true. One can only speculate on this plainly empirical matter.

10 Metaphysical Bullshit

As mentioned in the Introduction, although metaphysics has made an impressive comeback over the past half-century, there are still a great many philosophers today who think it is bullshit, under numerous precisifications of "That's just bullshit" so that it's a negative assessment and doesn't apply to most philosophy, so it singles out metaphysics as particularly worse off than most other fields of philosophy.[3] On Frankfurt's (2005) conception of bullshit, a person who makes bullshit statements is *not interested* in whether her statement is true or false. Perhaps some philosophers who accuse metaphysics of being "bullshit" think that metaphysicians aren't even *interested* in truth. This is an obvious psychological falsehood, however, and not worth responding to. But there are conceptions of bullshit that are more relevant to the accusations thrown at metaphysics, ones that preserve the basic idea that metaphysics is significantly worse off compared to other areas of philosophy. For instance, perhaps it's bullshit because it consists of pseudo-problems, while other philosophical areas don't have that problem to nearly the degree metaphysics does. Or maybe it's because it can't produce any results, whereas non-bullshit areas can and do. Or it's because metaphysics alone is pervasively tied to hopelessly confused language that makes its putative theses lack truth-value. Or it's because metaphysicians take seriously obviously false claims and waste prodigious amounts of energy evaluating obviously true claims. Regarding this last idea, we are familiar with the fact that many metaphysical problems generate bizarre philosophical views, such as the view that one thing can be numerically identical with many things, the view that there are millions of ordinary trees where common sense says there is just one tree, or the idea that there are no trees whatsoever. One could easily suspect that it is a good example of a bullshit pseudo-problem – and that metaphysics itself is bullshit, given that it is rife with such problems. These accusations can have all sorts of relations to one another. Anyone who talks to a diverse group of philosophers has heard the BS complaint many times, even if it's uncertain (or even underdetermined) what exactly is being said.

Here are the three theses regarding metaphysics and bullshit:

---

[3] Portions of this section are from my 2021 *Synthese* article.

T_5:   If a philosophical problem generates a true CD each disjunct of which is philosophically counterintuitive, then that problem is not bullshit, in most of the senses of "bullshit" used in common accusations such as "Today's metaphysics is just bullshit."

T_6:   Many metaphysical problems generate true CDs each of whose disjuncts are philosophically counterintuitive.

T_7:   If T_5 and T_6 are true, then metaphysics isn't "bullshit" in most of the senses of "bullshit" used in common accusations such as "Today's metaphysics is just bullshit."

T_5 is a conditional claim, so we have to assess it appropriately. Let's suppose its generalization is false. It follows that a philosophical field of inquiry includes a problem that has been used to generate a *true* CD each disjunct of which is highly counterintuitive. I think that proves that the problem itself is pretty important – hardly "bullshit." After all, the philosophical problem provides all the materials one needs to *prove* something, which is an accomplishment in itself; and the thing it proves shows (through entailment) that some *highly counterintuitive* claim is true, which is another accomplishment. Moreover, the fact that the disjuncts are highly counterintuitive shows that it is perfectly appropriate that metaphysics includes (i) taking seriously claims that are highly counterintuitive and (ii) careful evaluations of claims that are "obviously" true (recall that (i) and (ii) were cited as potential problems with metaphysics). I'm unsure of all the things meant by "That philosophical problem is bullshit" so that it's negative and indicates that the problem is significantly worse off than other philosophical problems, but I think these remarks count heavily against at least most BS accusations.

Regarding T_6: Similar proofs of other true CDs can be constructed in the same fashion using materials from other metaphysical chestnuts such as the Statue–Clay problem, the Ship of Theseus problem, the Tibbles–Tib problem, van Inwagen's argument for incompatibilism, paradoxes about color tokens, and so on. This is not to say that the CD disjuncts in question are, in each case, as philosophically counterintuitive as those for the Sorites, Liar, or Problem of the Many. They aren't, but that hardly matters to the truth of T_6. Further, some of those problems are a mixture of metaphysics and other fields such as the philosophy of language, mind, or logic, but that hardly matters either: Many philosophical problems having nothing to do with metaphysics are a mix. If the philosophical significance of metaphysics lies *mainly* in the philosophy of language and logic, well, that is fine; that hardly suggests that metaphysics is bullshit.

Roughly put, what is needed to prove a surprising CD is this: a philosophy problem that under consistent disambiguation generates a set of highly intuitive claims such that, when subject to highly intuitively truth-preserving inference rules, can be used to derive the negation of a highly intuitive claim. Those conditions are satisfied for problems in other fields of philosophy as well, thereby showing that those problems aren't bullshit either: Curry's Paradox, the Grelling–Nelson paradox, the No–No paradox, the Paradox of the Knower, Fitch's paradox, the Surprise Exam, the St. Petersburg paradox, the Suspense paradox, Russell's paradox, Yablo's paradox, the Dogmatism paradox, the Preface paradox, the relativity of simultaneity paradox, and so on.

One could object to T_7 on the grounds that the proofs of the CDs do nothing to *solve* any controversial philosophical problem. For instance, even after accepting the proofs we don't thereby come to know whether dialetheism is true, whether epistemicism is true, whether the simple inference rules in question are truth-preserving, whether trees are composed of chemical atoms, and so forth. I agree. But that fact fails to suggest that T_7 is false. The theses show that metaphysics isn't bullshit; they aren't intended to solve any philosophical problem other than the metaphilosophical one of "Is metaphysics bullshit?"

A much better objection to T_7 is that, even though I'm right that there are a bunch of non-bullshit problems in metaphysics, much of its unique jargon is so ill-defined that many discussions using that term are hopelessly muddled. The key terms in the objection are "much" and "many," since using "some" would hardly distinguish metaphysics from other areas of philosophy. Now, there is nothing in this Element that rules out the possibility that the problem of jargon-muddle is significantly worse in metaphysics than other areas. However, the onus is on the critic to make the comparative point. That would be a large project.

With these theses T_5–T_7 I'm not merely saying that metaphysics has some philosophically important problems. I'm saying that (i) starting from *several* metaphysical problems we can construct (ii) *proofs* that (iii) establish the existence of *philosophically counterintuitive truths* – although the oddity, as we have seen, is that we aren't sure which philosophically counterintuitive disjuncts of the CDs are the true ones. That should go a long way in showing, by concrete examples, that metaphysics isn't bullshit. Metaphysics might not be a shining city on a hill, filled with nothing but lovely, morally upstanding problems and issues, but it's not the slum many have accused it of being. Although I have not argued for the thesis here, I think that since metaphysics has (i)–(iii) going for it, and some other areas of philosophy do not, metaphysics is, to a certain extent, *further* from being bullshit than those other areas of philosophy. Metaphysics deserves our admiration, and not our mere tolerance.

11 Philosophical Progress and Philosophical Refutations of Common Sense

One occasionally encounters informal arguments of the following form: (i) All the offered solutions to such-and-such philosophical problem are anti-commonsensical in some respect. (ii) There's no reason to hope that we've overlooked a commonsensical solution. Thus, some anti-commonsensical theory is true (Schwitzgebel 2014, 2017). Both premises can be debated for eons. My argument will be similar but stronger.

However, what does "commonsensical" mean. Better yet, what *should* it mean, in order to have an interesting discussion about whether philosophy refutes "common sense"?

The term "commonsensical" admits of multiple readings, some of which are philosophically useful. One such useful reading relativizes to group and time, so "The Earth is round" is commonsensical for some groups and times (scientifically educated adults today) but not others (four-year-old children today, adults from 1000 BCE). The claim that modus ponens is truth-preserving is commonsensical for those who know logic but not to most other groups (*just* truth-preserving; in this Element, I make no use of stronger notions such as "truth-preserving in virtue of logical form"). In this section, a claim K is commonsensical at a time for a certain large community = virtually everyone in that community at that time who understands K well *either* already have a high degree of belief and credence in K *or* would have such belief and credence fairly quickly and easily if asked whether K is true. In this Element, I'm concerned with what counts as common sense amongst a particular community and time: contemporary philosophers, where the latter are almost entirely philosophy professors and advanced PhD students. Some clarifications of the definition of commonsensicality are in order.

First, the definition's second disjunct is meant to account for claims that people in the community have yet to judge. For instance, "Baseball is not played on Jupiter" and "$2.111 + 0.455 = 2.566$" are commonsensical for the community of competent adults today even though few of them have ever considered those two claims.

Second, the definition does not rely on the idea of a claim being *intuitive*. For instance, the definition does not count N, "There are twice as many positive integers as there are even positive integers," as commonsensical amongst philosophers. It's true that people who have learned a significant amount of transfinite number theory usually still have an intuition, of a sort, to accept N: If you put your mind in the right position, so to speak, N remains "intuitive." Similarly, a color scientist who is convinced that no ordinary objects are colored is disposed, in that intuition-sense, to think her new blouse is yellow. The claim N about transfinite numbers doesn't count as commonsensical for contemporary philosophers because, even though we can still feel the intuitive pull of N, the vast majority of us will reject it if asked to evaluate it, since a good portion of us have heard at least a bit about elementary transfinite number theory. Intuitively attractive ≠ commonsensical.

Third, a philosopher doesn't have to be a successful researcher on C in order to "understand C well," in the sense I'm using that phrase in the definition. For instance, I'm neither a logician nor a philosopher of logic but I understand modus ponens well. I've taught logic several times, I once took a class in the philosophy of logic, and I once studied the 1985 Van McGee article that proposed a counterexample (one that doesn't apply to the cases described in this Element, since they don't have conditionals as consequents of the material conditionals). When it comes to the Sorites SCs, I understand them well, since even though I haven't published a professional work on the topic, I've studied (not merely read) Williamson's (1994) book and taught the issue to many students. But when it comes to issues in philosophical ethics, I don't understand the relevant claims well, as I can barely teach a competent introductory course in ethics. Shame.

Some philosophers are convinced that nonformal philosophy has never, to date, refuted common sense. As a result of that belief, they usually make what I call the Moorean move (mentioned in the Introduction):

> When you encounter what you know to be a nonformal philosophical argument that goes counterintuitively against common sense, an epistemically rational thing to do (maybe the only rational thing to do) is retain your commonsensical belief and conclude that the argument is unsound – and this can be done independently of finding specific fault in the argument (which is not to say that you take yourself to have failed to find such fault).

G. E. Moore (1925), David Lewis (1973), Kit Fine (2001), Anil Gupta (2006), William Lycan (2001, 2019), Jonathan Schaffer (2009), and Thomas Kelly (2008) are representative philosophers who make the move and defend or assume its epistemic rationality; one also sees the move made a great many times in philosophical conversation. The Moorean move often gets made with respect to arguments for external world skepticism. However, one cannot reasonably restrict the Moorean move to those arguments – and in practice it certainly isn't so restricted. It would be bizarre to be confident enough in "He knows he has hands" to make the Moorean move but not confident enough to make the move for other commonsensical claims – such as "He has hands."

I think that once one has read widely in philosophy, one should be a bit suspicious about the Moorean move. In addition, once one is thoroughly familiar with the paradoxes in philosophy, one should be *highly* suspicious. More carefully, I think that *once one is familiar with the arguments against common sense constructed here*, then the Moorean move is no longer reasonable, assuming it ever was.

What we would like, when someone comes to one of us and claims that philosophy refutes common sense, is for this to happen:

> I was presented with argument X. I saw that X is a deductively sound philosophical argument. I also saw that X's conclusion is an anti-commonsensical claim.

That would be *beautiful*. I haven't given you that; sorry. Instead, this is what I made happen:

> I was presented with an argument X. I saw that X is a deductively sound philosophical argument. I also saw that X's conclusion starts with "At least one of the following half dozen or so anti-commonsensical claims is true." Unfortunately, I wasn't told which of the half dozen or so anti-commonsensical claims are true, but I saw that each is philosophically counterintuitive. So, the philosophy argument conclusively shows that *some* anti-commonsensical claim is true.

My X arguments are just what you expect: the arguments for the CDs. In each case, we have a nonformal philosophy argument that shows that common sense is mistaken – and although the argument doesn't tell us *exactly* where common sense is mistaken, it does narrow it down quite a bit, to some quite fundamental commonsensical claims (the disjuncts). That is thesis T_8:

T_8:   There are non-formal philosophy arguments that show that common sense is mistaken – and although the arguments don't tell us exactly where common sense is mistaken, they do narrow it down quite a bit, to some quite fundamental commonsensical claims.

There is little profit in fighting over the best way(s) of making "x refutes y" precise, but for my money, the proofs of the CDs have what it takes to satisfy at least some reasonable and philosophically interesting precisifications of "philosophical argument that refutes a portion of common sense."

One might object to the significance, but not truth, of T_8 by claiming that the true CDs never have true disjuncts that go against "ordinary, everyday" common sense, such as "There are eight trees on my property line," "Mom knows you bought a motorcycle," and "Fatima believes her boyfriend is cheating on her." Instead, the true disjuncts will be philosophical claims like these (from the Sorites and Liar CDs):

- At least one of the simplest sentential inference rules isn't truth-preserving when applied to pairs of very simple sentences.
- At least some of the middle SCs aren't even disjunctions.
- There are a great many true contradictions coming from ordinary sentences (not weird, liar-type ones), even assuming a paraconsistent logic.
- At least some of the sentences expressing SD_1–SD_3 are true in this Element but false in ordinary discourse, despite not containing philosophical jargon and contrary to my explicit interpretative instructions.
- We can neither stipulate that "Alf" will refer to "Alf isn't true" nor use a definite description such as "The third indented sentence on page 774" to set up the reference for "Alf."
- Alf isn't true but "Alf isn't true" isn't true; or "Alf isn't true" is true but it's not the case that Alf isn't true.

However, I have no idea why one might think that "ordinary, everyday" common sense is forever immune to philosophical refutation, once (i) one realizes that science has already refuted parts of it and (ii) one has insisted that philosophy has already refuted fundamental claims about meaning, elementary logic, and/or truth (since one admits that the true CD disjuncts have those three topics at targets).

My next thesis:

T_9:   The arguments for and agreement regarding T_1 and T_2 constitute significant philosophical progress.

I implicitly quantify over interesting and plausible precisifications of "philosophical progress."

As far as I know, no first-order philosophy problem is solved by any of my arguments. Even so, what we learn from the CDs is that a great many of our most confidently held and truly fundamental beliefs – about truth, meaning, or the ordinary empirical world – are false. I consider that a real result. Roughly put, the fact that T_8 is true is enough to show that T_9 is true.

12 The Philosophical Significance of Philosophical Counterintuitiveness

In 2018, the baseball pitcher Jacob deGrom won the Cy Young award for best pitcher in the National League of professional baseball. The claim "deGrom should have won the Cy Young award" is counterintuitive amongst people who formed their standards for judging baseball excellence by watching baseball in the decades before 2000. Back then, most everyone judged pitching performance primarily with won-loss records, and deGrom's 2018 won-loss record was just 10–9. If you have kept up with developments about how to judge pitching performance, "deGrom should have won the Cy Young award" is not at all counterintuitive despite his unimpressive won-loss record. You might not think the deGrom claim is actually true, since other pitchers had comparably impressive performances in 2018, but you would hardly find the deGrom claim *counterintuitive*. Unkindly put, that sentence is counterintuitive today only for people who are morons about baseball.

You might, if you are unkind, say something similar about philosophy.

The percentage of (informed) epistemicists amongst philosophers is tiny. The percentage of (again, informed) epistemicists amongst philosophers of language is higher. The percentage amongst philosophers of language who work on the philosophical issues about vagueness is even higher. Finally, the percentage amongst those whose primary research focus over many years is vagueness is yet higher. The more you know about vagueness, the more attractive epistemicism is.

You might think this has happened because advanced work on vagueness is wonderfully on track for truth; alternatively, you might think this is due to a pernicious assumption infecting the ranks of otherwise excellent philosophers of language. This is not my fight.

Instead, my point is that there is a reasonable objection lying in wait here. One might think that although the CD disjuncts are "philosophically counterintuitive" according to my definition – so my theses are *true* – this fact is not philosophically significant. And the reason it's not philosophically significant is that epistemicism is counterintuitive only for philosophers who are morons about vagueness (that is the unkind bit). So the objection runs: "Sure, the CD disjuncts are counterintuitive, but really that's just because of the great diversity of philosophical backgrounds amongst philosophers." So, isn't there something wrong, or at least provincial, about my proofs of philosophical counterintuitiveness, since they target only nonexperts? Why should we care about whether a claim is counterintuitive amongst nonexperts? Perhaps this Element's theses are true but not philosophically significant. The horror.

I have a five-part reply to this *Significance Objection*. And yes, each part is important.

First, applicability. This objection requires the "true experts" finding P not counterintuitive even while the unwashed masses of philosophers find P counterintuitive. I chose epistemicism in articulating the objection because it's arguable that it fits the scenario pretty well – at least today (it certainly didn't a few decades ago; the objection fails then). But a quick glance at the disjuncts of various CDs (both the Sorites and others) shows that the scenario simply doesn't apply to most disjuncts. Thus, even if the objection is sound, it applies only to a few disjuncts. And what happens when it does apply? See point five below, the killer one.

Second, historical variability. Even when the scenario does apply at a time, expert opinion is a fickle thing. Perhaps "true expert" opinion finds disjunct D not counterintuitive in 2021 but did find it counterintuitive in 1991 and will find it counterintuitive in 2051. It's not hard to think of many precedents, such as panpsychism. Or epistemicism for that matter! Hence, the Significance Objection may have fleeting application.

Third, cherry-picking the experts. "The true experts on vagueness find epistemicism not counterintuitive." "Okay, but how do we determine who an expert is on vagueness?" "Well, for starters, they should take epistemicism very seriously." Don't laugh; I have had virtually this very conversation. The circularity might well be benign, or merely apparent, but it's worth flagging as a potential problem.

Fourth, the significance of the general counterintuitiveness. Even if we restrict our attention to the philosophers who find the disjuncts counterintuitive, there certainly are enough of them – and enough that are deserving of our respect as fully competent philosophers – that theses T_1–T_9 are philosophically significant regardless of what the "true experts" happen to think at a particular time.

Fifth, the origin of expert non-counterintuitiveness. The reason epistemicism is no longer counterintuitive amongst experts is ... the Sorites paradox. In general, what often *makes* the expert/nonexpert divide regarding counterintuitiveness genuine and long-lasting is extended reflection on the paradox, by the experts alone. This is important for my project due to the nature of my theses. I locate the philosophical significance of the paradoxes in theses T_3–T_9 (thus far; I haven't even gotten to the controversial epistemic thesis T_{10} that I defend in subsequent sections).

T_3:   The arguments for T_1 and T_2 are knockdown arguments in at least most of the senses of "knockdown argument" used in common accusations such as "Unlike the sciences, philosophy has no knockdown arguments."

T_4:   We agree that the CDs are true and their disjuncts are philosophically counterintuitive.

T_5:   If a philosophical problem generates a true CD each disjunct of which is philosophically counterintuitive, then that problem is not bullshit, in most of the senses of "bullshit" used in common accusations such as "Today's metaphysics is just bullshit."

T_6: Many metaphysical problems generate true CDs each of whose disjuncts are philosophically counterintuitive.

T_7: If T_5 and T_6 are true, then metaphysics isn't "bullshit" in most of the senses of "bullshit" used in common accusations such as "Today's metaphysics is just bullshit."

T_8: There are nonformal philosophy arguments that show that common sense is mistaken – and although the arguments don't tell us exactly where common sense is mistaken, they do narrow it down quite a bit, to some quite fundamental commonsensical claims.

T_9: The arguments for and agreement regarding T_1 and T_2 constitute significant philosophical progress.

If the expert/nonexpert counterintuitiveness divide exists for some disjuncts, often enough it was reflection on the corresponding philosophical paradox that *generated* that divide. To that extent, the paradox is philosophically significant. Hence, if the Significance Objection shows anything, it shows that when the expert/nonexpert divide exists, that amounts to a sign of the significance of the paradox (which is not to say that the theses aren't significant; my other four remarks still hold).

My experience in the profession suggests that a fair number of philosophers are almost desperate to argue, "Oh, that famous philosophical problem is just a waste of time. It's a blind alley when it comes to philosophical insight." It's not nice to say this, but I think the reason many (not all) of these philosophers are so dismissive of certain traditional problems is that they realize, at least dimly, that they have nothing remotely insightful to say about them – and that realization is embarrassing to them. They are secretly a little ashamed that they are clueless about what to say about the philosophical problems in question. As a consequence, they want the problems to *just go away and leave us alone.* This suspicion is little more than armchair psychology though; so, evaluate it with that in mind.

I suspect that their position, when made precise, entails that the optimal way(s) to respond to the philosophical problems in question will not include endorsing any philosophically significant claims. After all, the problems are mere pseudo-problems according to them. However, we have seen that they are wrong, at least when it comes to the Sorites, Liar, and Problem of the Many. There is *no* way to respond to those paradoxes without embracing a philosophically counterintuitive claim. These philosophers will be wrong for other philosophical problems that can be put in paradox form and generate true CDs with philosophically counterintuitive disjuncts.

13 The Three Doxastic Responses to the Doxastically Distressing Disjunctions

Let's assume you have accepted that the CDs are true – since you are a lover of the good, true, and beautiful. So, you accept that some of those philosophically counterintuitive disjuncts are true too. Which ones do you think are true? More to the point, do you think you can *trust your judgment* about this matter of figuring out which counterintuitive disjuncts are the true ones? If you think you can, are you an arrogant fool? I'm joking ... sort of.

It's not surprising that the typical philosopher who is aware she isn't a genius but is wise will not have many philosophical opinions that she knows to be highly controversial amongst the relevant specialists. But what about thinking that there are trees in North America? Or that modus ponens is truth-preserving? Or that certain simple sentences of English are disjunctions? I will now argue that most philosophers must, if they are wise and have a deep understanding of the panoply of philosophical paradoxes (brought about by reading this Element, for instance), suspend judgment on even those claims. I realize that this is an extreme thesis, but the paradoxes are extreme in their epistemic consequences.

Certain comparisons are helpful in order to see the situation that applies to those of us who have got this far in the Element. For instance, there are many entertaining pseudo-proofs of claims such as "0 = 1." When one first encounters them, one might, depending on one's familiarity with algebra, not be able to see the mistake in the proof (they often divide by zero at some point). Even so, one can be reasonable in sticking with one's prior belief that $0 \neq 1$ and concluding that the proof is mistaken somewhere even if one hasn't yet found the error. People often adopt the same response to Zeno's paradoxes.

What one does *not* do with the entertaining pseudo-proofs is this: stick with one's prior belief that $0 \neq 1$, accept each premise in the puzzling proof of $0 = 1$ as true, accept that the inferences are all truth-preserving, and accept that there is no equivocation or other semantic funny business going on. Nope! Instead, one concludes that *there is a mistake somewhere*. That's precisely what we are doing with the philosophical paradoxes – and the CDs are summaries of the only options for the mistake.

One might hesitate to endorse the disjunctions out of concern that there might be some crucial ambiguity that ruins the soundness of the proofs for them. If the disjuncts contained unclear philosophical jargon such as "phenomenal consciousness," "free will," or the like, then this could be a serious worry depending on the details. But the disjuncts we have looked at have no such jargon. In addition, we have covered contextual issues repeatedly.

Alternatively, one might have a vague suspicion that "true" has some pluralistic semantics to it that ruins the proofs of the CDs, or maybe takes away their significance, or something similar. But all the Sorites SCs, for instance, have the same topic (people being poor and having certain amounts of financial worth), so cases of truth pluralism or views about there being different kinds of truth won't help (e.g. Pedersen and Wright 2013).

If one has lost all confidence in one's abilities to discover truth, then I suppose one could be reasonable in failing to accept the CDs even after competently seeing how their supporting arguments pass any reasonable test for soundness. But if one is so suspicious of the CDs that one denies or even merely suspends judgment on their truth – even after going through the proofs of them – then how can one be so confident that the disjuncts are all false?

This is not to say that the wise philosopher must *believe* the disjunctions. It's only to say that she will believe them *provided* she would be confident enough in her judgment to disbelieve one or more of the disjuncts.

In any case, regardless of whether the philosopher who has read this far epistemically *should* believe that the CDs are true and have philosophically counterintuitive disjuncts, I will make five *assumptions* regarding the epistemology of "our" responses to the CDs.

A1: We accept that the CDs in this Element are true, based on our careful evaluation of them.

A2: We accept that each disjunct of each CD is philosophically counterintuitive, again based on our careful evaluation of them.

A3: We believe that there are other CDs, from other paradoxes, that are true and that have only philosophically counterintuitive disjuncts.

A4: We have taken on the task of answering the question, "What are the truth-values of the disjuncts of the CDs?"

A5: We have taken on the task of answering the question, "Is my judgment reliable when answering the previous question?"

In other words, I'm wondering what we readers of this book should do about the CDs and their disjuncts, now that we've seen and carefully thought about them and are attuned to the possibility that we might not be reliable in evaluating them.

I'm not saying that the epistemic position of other philosophers, who don't satisfy those assumptions, is uninteresting. Instead, I am merely focusing on one interesting subclass of the general situation in which one might retain one's beliefs after encountering arguments against those beliefs – arguments that one sees are quite strong.

For each CD, there are three responses for the philosopher who satisfies our assumptions. Keep in mind that every disjunct is recognized to be philosophically counterintuitive.

Inconsistency: Believe the disjunction (because we proved it) but disbelieve every disjunct. This person embraces inconsistency: she sides with common sense in disbelieving every counterintuitive disjunct, she sides with rationality in accepting the CD (as per assumption 1), and, because she is appropriately self-aware, she recognizes her inconsistency but accepts it (a sixth assumption if you will).

Confident: Believe the disjunction (because we proved it) and believe at least one disjunct. This person is confident she has found the true disjunct(s).

Cautious: Believe the disjunction (because we proved it), don't go so far as to believe any of the counterintuitive disjuncts, but don't disbelieve all of them either (she can disbelieve *some* of them). This person is cautious: she accepts that the disjunction is true, but she refuses to endorse any of the disjuncts, and she's consistent enough to not disbelieve all of them. Hence, she suspends judgment on some disjuncts (in one sense of "suspend judgment").

The reader can verify that, for any given CD, the three responses are mutually exclusive and logically exhaustive; there are no alternatives (assuming the agent believes the disjunction).

One might take different responses for different CDs. In the next three sections, I argue that the Cautious response is wiser than the other two.

T_{10}:   The Cautious response is wiser than the other two responses, for philosophers satisfying assumptions A1–A5.

I will *not* be able to offer convincing arguments for this thesis, as I don't have the space, ability, or conviction. But I can highlight many of the relevant considerations, as food for thought.

I focus on wise responses rather than epistemically rational responses. It's at least debatable that the bar for the latter is pretty low. I'm one of those philosophers who suspects that knowledge and epistemically rational belief are a lot less intellectual or even epistemically impressive than the vast majority of philosophers have thought (even for "reflective" knowledge). If one assumes a super-high standard for knowledge or rational belief, then it will not be hard to use that assumption in arguing that the philosopher aware of the truth of the CDs doesn't *know* (or have a rational belief regarding) which disjuncts are true, even if she has the right true beliefs. I will not be going down that route for two reasons: I don't make that assumption and I'm not even going to broach the subject of a philosopher's knowledge of the true disjuncts.

Instead, I start with the idea that the bar for wisdom is relatively high. I would like to know what the wise response to the paradoxes is. In addition, I want to allow for the possibility that two not insignificantly different doxastic responses X1 and X2 to the same event might be epistemically rational but X1 is significantly epistemically better than X2. I do not address any particular theory of wisdom, either absolute or comparative.

14 The Inconsistency Response

This philosopher looks at the philosophically counterintuitive disjuncts and thinks that surely they are all false. But what about the disjunction? Well, she says, it's true. Because she's no fool, she recognizes and accepts her inconsistency. "Deal with it," she advises.

The Inconsistency response is at least somewhat familiar from the Preface paradox in which one finds oneself strongly disposed to believe each of theses T_1 –T_{100} ("Each of my theses is true") but also roughly equally disposed to believe ($\sim T_1$ v $\sim T_2$ v ... v $\sim T_{100}$) ("Well, surely either the first is false, or maybe the second, or maybe the third, etc.") and be aware of the obvious inconsistency. Some philosophers (e.g. Kyburg 1961) have thought that one can be rational in believing all 101 theses (the 100 Ts plus the disjunction of their negations) while being aware of the inconsistency (so there aren't odd circumstances that make it difficult for one to see the inconsistency, such as those in Frege's puzzle (Frege 1892/1997), Kripke's puzzle (Kripke 1979), multiple personality disorder, etc.).

If one has only a dim grasp of the concept of inconsistency, then I suppose one can be reasonable in admitting one's inconsistency. And even if one has a firm grasp of it – as a philosopher will – one can be reasonable in admitting one's inconsistency for *enormous* disjunctions (e.g. the disjunction of practically all of one's beliefs). However, if one has the firm grasp of the concept of inconsistency, and one sees that there is a *small* number of disjuncts, then it seems to me that one is not being wise but foolish and evasive. The philosopher who writes an essay that defends just a half dozen theses, who believes each of them but also believes the disjunction of their negations while aware of the inconsistency in his views, isn't being wise at all. For the paradoxes, the number of disjuncts is similarly low. Even if there are degrees of responding wisely (so A's response can be wiser than B's, which is wiser than C's) and the Inconsistency response has some nonzero amount or degree of wisdom, the other responses are significantly wiser than the Inconsistency response.

15 The Confident Response

This philosopher accepts the soundness of the proof of the disjunction and thinks she has found the true disjunct. Consistency is attained.

But recall that the epistemic situation we are examining is *not* that of a philosopher responding to *just* the Sorites paradox, *or* the Liar paradox, *or* the Problem of the Many, *or* Tibbles–Tib, and so on. No, I have in mind a more restricted situation: someone (like you and myself) who satisfies assumptions A1–A5. You and I have the task of responding to a *bunch* of CDs. You probably aren't aware of the details of each one (unless you have done a lot of work inspired by this Element); no such devotion is necessary to get the epistemic problem loaded. For instance, I have worked out in detail only several of them, but I have sketched a couple of others and – the key point – I know that there are more disjunctions awaiting me. I estimate that you and I are faced with dozens of disjuncts from a bunch of CDs, each disjunct philosophically counterintuitive, and yet we know that some of those disjuncts are true. It is not an intelligent response to the problem posed by the doxastically distressing disjunctions to focus on *just* the Liar, for instance, and offer one's favorite solution to just it. I mean, the well-informed philosopher has a significantly larger task.

I suspect the following situation will be common. After one has seen the philosophically counterintuitive disjuncts, call them the Ds, in one particular CD, one looks at D_4, say, and thinks to oneself something that can be captured with the following inner speech:

> Well sure, D_4 is initially counterintuitive – like each of the Ds is. There are good reasons to think D_4 is false; no doubt about it. But the reasons to think it's false are definitely weaker than the reasons to think the other Ds are false. When you add up all the evidence, D_4 is definitely more plausible than any of the other Ds. Although D_4 is indeed implausible, it is *less implausible* than the others, if you will. So we should conclude that it's the true one.

How often is this response wise for the philosopher who is familiar with many paradoxes (satisfying our five assumptions)?

On the one hand, we philosophers make doxastic moves similar to that one all the time when faced with a plainly valid argument for a conclusion that we disbelieve – and the move is often quite reasonable, or so we can plausibly allow for the sake of argument. For comparison, suppose we think C is false but later accept that $\{P_A, P_B, P_C\} \vDash C$. Suppose further that we see that, while P_C is at least somewhat plausible, it is not plausible enough for the argument to succeed because it's significantly less plausible than ~C. That is, we are much more confident in the falsehood of the conclusion than the truth of one of the premises. In effect, we are recognizing what we take to be *a true disjunction of individually initially counterintuitive claims*, ($\sim P_A$ v $\sim P_B$ v $\sim P_C$ v C), and we are judging $\sim P_C$ to be the most plausible/least implausible one. In such a situation, rejecting P_C and retaining belief in ~C is wise. The comparison with doxastically distressing disjunctions is obvious from the italics.

Assume there are many philosophers who satisfy assumptions A1–A5 and take the Confident response. They will typically fall into one of four groups, G1–G4. In what follows, I do not aim for completeness; I aim to briefly examine the categories that philosophers usually find themselves in.

G1: Philosophers who rely on counterintuitiveness comparisons in order to figure out which disjuncts are the true ones *and* who never found the eventually believed disjuncts to be counterintuitive. That is, they look at the disjuncts of some particular CD, admit that each one is typically found counterintuitive by many philosophers, but then they judge at least one of them to *not* strike them as counterintuitive. So, they judge that one to be true. They do this over and over, for various CDs.

I know it's not a nice thing to say, but I think that many philosophers in G1 are guilty of either of two mistakes: one, misjudging the disjuncts, not seeing that they really are quite extreme; or two, caught in self-deception, since they are lying to themselves about the counterintuitiveness of the disjuncts they endorse. The first mistake can be epistemically if not professionally blameless. Philosophy is hard, after all. The latter mistake often is a consequence of what I pointed out in Section 12: A fair number of philosophers are almost desperate to diminish the importance of famous philosophical problems that they implicitly know they have been defeated by. As I asserted earlier, these philosophers want the problems to *just go away and leave us alone*.

But suppose a philosopher in G1 isn't subject to those mistakes. What then?

If you are in G1, you truly don't find a certain disjunct counterintuitive even though you understand it thoroughly, and you judge it to be the true one based on your counterintuitiveness comparison, then you should realize that you are relying on a judgment of counterintuitiveness *that is rejected by the clear majority of competent philosophers*. For instance, suppose with respect to the Sorites CD you think it's not counterintuitive to hold that "Everyone is poor" is true in ordinary discourse. Surely, you realize that your position here, on counterintuitiveness, is rejected by the vast majority of competent philosophers. Some philosophers might agree with you that the disjunct in question is true, but even so the clear majority of them will admit that it's counterintuitive – contrary to your position. So that raises the question, "Are my judgments about counter-intuitiveness that are rejected by most competent philosophers like me reliable?" This is nothing like the mere one-on-one peer disagreement case, since we are dealing with large numbers of philosophers, many of whom are your recognized epistemic superiors on the relevant issues. For reasons I have given elsewhere (Frances 2020), these "minority" judgments are usually irrational.

G2: Philosophers who rely on counterintuitiveness comparisons in order to figure out which disjuncts are the true ones and admit that the eventually believed disjuncts are counterintuitive. That is, in order to figure out which disjunct is true, they do a comparison: The disjunct that is least counterintuitive they judge to be the true one, provided that disjunct wins the contest by a big margin. They do this over and over, for various CDs.

These philosophers admit that the disjuncts are counterintuitive; so, they avoid the problems with G1. They have a different problem, however. On the one hand, they realize that some of the philosophical claims they thought *highly counterintuitive* are actually true. On the other hand, they realize that they are now relying on their comparative judgments of counterintuitiveness in order to figure out which disjuncts are true. But once one admits that one's counter-intuitiveness judgments get clearly fundamentally important claims dead wrong, it's not wise to rely on those judgments, or extremely similar judgments, when trying to figure out which disjuncts are true.

The key here is "clearly fundamentally important." To see this, consider an objection to the preceding argument.

> Yes, I admit that I thought disjunct D was counterintuitive and false, and now I'm saying it's true. So, my judgments about the falsehood of counterintuitive claims aren't perfect! But being wrong once hardly means that my judgments about counterintuitive claims are *unreliable*.

There are two major problems with this objection.

First, there is the *Numbers argument*. The wise philosopher will see that the truth of several disjuncts, from several true CDs, will entail that *a great many* of her prior philosophical views and presuppositions are false (e.g. many of the commonsensical ones whose negations are entailed by the true disjuncts). For most if not all of the disjuncts, the inference from "Disjunct D is true" to "I have been wrong about a colossal number of related claims" is required. For instance, if she judges that she was wrong about SD_1 or SD_2 from the Sorites, then it should be obvious to her that she has been wrong about an enormous number of closely related claims (since the Sorites paradox can be run on an enormous number and variety of claims). She will then, because she is thinking things through, see that her philosophical judgment has not been trustworthy because it's been unreliable. But if that is the case, and she is wise, then she should not trust her comparative counterintuitiveness judgments regarding the disjuncts.

Second, there is the *Credence argument*. The wise philosopher will see that the truth of several disjuncts will show, through entailment, that many of her prior philosophical beliefs *with the highest credence* turned out to be false. She will then, because she is thinking things through, see that her philosophical judgment has not been trustworthy. But if that is the case, and she is wise, then she should not trust her judgment regarding comparative counterintuitiveness judgments regarding the disjuncts.

Regarding the Credence argument, suppose I work in the philosophy of language. I am highly confident that a certain thesis S_1 is true (perhaps S_1 is "We can use 'The third sentence on page 774' to fix the reference of a new proper name"). So, I have a firm belief in S_1. Of course, I have other opinions in the philosophy of language, on a variety of topics: I think theses S_2–S_{10} are true as well. But I am significantly less certain of those beliefs than my belief in S_1; I think my overall evidence for S_1 considerably exceeds that for most if not all of S_2–S_{10}. But then, to my surprise, I encounter what I see to be a true CD one of whose disjuncts is $\sim S_1$. (More likely, I see that I can easily construct a CD that has $\sim S_1$ as a disjunct.) After judging the disjuncts, I come to think S_1 is false (so $\sim S_1$ is the true disjunct). But how can I continue trusting my old judgments about the philosophy of language theses that I had already admitted were significantly *less* supported than S_1?

It's no good to reply, "Well, I've received excellent evidence against S_1, not the others; so why should I give up my beliefs in the others?" You have also received excellent evidence against the reliability of your judgment regarding philosophical theses in the philosophy of language. Deciding that S_1 is false might correct one mistake you made – assuming, what is controversial, that you found the true disjunct – but it remains the case that you have decent evidence that your philosophy of language judgment is not trustworthy. And as the Numbers argument showed, it's not just *one* mistake.

Perhaps it's worth reminding the reader that my thesis is that the Confident response is not *wise* compared to the Cautious response. I'm not saying that it is irrational by professional or other standards (or no standards).

But what if, as a matter of objective fact, a philosopher's comparative counterintuitiveness judgments regarding the disjuncts is highly reliable? Suppose further that she aligns her beliefs with that reliable "faculty." Are her subsequent doxastic moves with regard to the disjuncts wise?

I don't think so, for the reasons I just gave. But suppose I'm wrong. All that means is that a *small percentage* of philosophers are reliable as described. We know that the percentage must be small given the wild diversity in judgment regarding the disjuncts.

G3: Philosophers who rely on *expert assessment* of comparative evidential strength of disjuncts. They are experts on all the disjuncts and use that expertise to allegedly discover that such-and-such disjunct, despite striking many philosophers as counterintuitive, is significantly better supported by the available evidence than the other disjuncts. They do this over and over, for various CDs.

There are several problems here, including those revealed by the Numbers and Credence arguments, but I will just point out the simplest one: Most of us are not experts on more than a few disjuncts in the various CDs. Sure, John Hawthorne and Tim Williamson have that kind of wide expertise, but you aren't them, are you? Hence, even if the philosophers in G3 are reasonable in their judgments regarding which disjuncts are true, there aren't many people in G3.

G4: Philosophers who rely on *admittedly nonexpert assessment* of comparative evidential strength of disjuncts. They are amateurs on some of the disjuncts and use their own knowledge, nonexpert as that is, to allegedly discover that such-and-such disjunct, despite striking many philosophers as counterintuitive, is significantly better supported by the available evidence than the other disjuncts. They do this over and over, for various CDs.

Ummm . . . why would one be confident in one's assessment of the comparative strength of evidence when one *admits* that one is an *amateur* on the relevant topics – ones for which expert assessment is nowhere near consensus? Why think that your amateur assessment of a profoundly controversial set of issues is reliable? It might be reasonable to implicitly assume reliability if one hasn't thought about it, but you have; you are reading this. For you, it is unwise to think your assessment is reliable – at least, it is if one realizes one's amateur status and recognizes how controversial the relevant issues are, even amongst specialists. And once again, the Numbers and Credence arguments apply to G4 as much as they did to G3 and G2.

16 The Cautious Response

The first two responses are usually unwise for most philosophers aware of the truth of many doxastically distressing disjunctions. As far as I've determined, there isn't anything epistemically wrong with the Cautious response. And if there is, which is a possibility worth taking seriously (again, philosophy is awfully hard), that would be yet another paradox to deal with. I can live with that result!

The argument for the superiority of the Cautious response is roughly this: (a) the other two responses are usually unwise, for the reasons I gave in the previous two sections; (b) the three responses are logically exhaustive and mutually exclusive; (c) there isn't good reason to think the Cautious response is unwise; so, (d) the Cautious response wins. The rest of this section defends (c) but hardly goes into any detail, as I'm up against a word limit.

There are at least two types of situations in which one suspends judgment on a claim after extensive attention and evaluation. First, you are convinced that the pro and con evidence is about balanced; in this case, one suspends *as the result of conviction* (this includes the case of thinking there is no evidence either way). Second, you see that you're in way over your head, and you can't even make the balance judgment. In the latter case, you say to yourself, "Wait a minute. I don't know *what* the hell to think about this." This is suspension *due to recognized confusion*, not conviction. I suspect that in most cases the philosopher who takes the Cautious response finds herself in that recognized state of confusion after contemplating the epistemic consequences of the disjuncts.

I have restricted our attention to philosophers who satisfy the five assumptions A1–A5. The first two involve belief:

A1:   We accept that the CDs in this book are true, based on our careful evaluation of them.

A2:   We accept that each disjunct of each CD is philosophically counterintuitive, again based on our careful evaluation of them.

Some philosophers are so cautious as to not satisfy these (taking a "Super Cautious" response). Frankly, I'm not even sure if I do. The arguments for the CDs look strong to me, but I've been suckered by so many clever yet flawed philosophical arguments that I have a serious worry, based on induction, that those arguments are fatally flawed (i.e. flaws that cannot be repaired while establishing the same, or approximately the same, conclusions). I *do* think those arguments are about as strong as any in philosophy (I flatter myself). But as a consequence of that "serious worry," I end up suspending on an incredibly wide swath of claims. I suspend judgment *not as the result of accepting an argument*, not even the ones in this book. Instead, I look at all the relevant arguments, realize I'm out of my depth, and *back off*, in the direction opposite of conviction.

A philosopher could attempt to figure out what credences she epistemically should have in the disjuncts and disjunctions, based on all her evidence, and *perhaps* there is a clear answer to that question. With all the evidence she has regarding everything that might be thought (or perhaps known) to be relevant, maybe there is a unique set of maximally epistemically rational doxastic attitudes for her to have regarding the operative claims. Or, if uniqueness of rational credence on an evidence base is false (so there is no unique set), perhaps there is a narrow band of maximally rational attitudes to have. Maybe we can delete "maximally" as well. But even under those optimistic assumptions, *if it is very difficult for her to figure out what those rational attitudes are* – which I think is the case here, assuming we have a typical real-life philosopher at hand – then the wise person suspends judgment regarding the body of confusing claims. Perhaps someday she'll figure out what beliefs and credences to have based on the overall evidence; in the meantime, the wise philosopher suspends judgment.

Her final step is to realize that, if she is going to suspend judgment on almost all of those disjuncts – which strike her to be as roughly likely to be false as almost any claim she has ever encountered – then she should suspend judgment on a great many other claims, although she won't be sure how far to spread her belief-suspension. She ends up with a kind of extremely widespread (but indeterminate in extent) suspension of belief, under one precisification of "belief" (under an action-guidance precisification, she still has plenty of beliefs, but that's only because she has to act in order to live).

Some philosophers, at least in conversation, think that it's almost psychologically impossible to suspend judgment on highly anti-commonsensical claims such as the disjuncts. If they are right, then we can't take the Cautious (or Super Cautious) response.

However, it's not hard to see how one could suspend judgment on almost everything for reasons that have nothing to do with abstract philosophical argument – which shows that the alleged psychological impossibility just doesn't exist. For instance, suppose one lives in a society in which the media have consistently and persistently over the last year conveyed all of the following to the public, with appropriate documentation and whistleblower revelations: BIVs (brains in vats) have been created; a team of mad scientists rules most of the world; top secret documents have been leaked that detail plans for massive kidnapping and BIVing; impenetrable 1,000-square-mile complexes of laboratories have been set up in the wilds of Canada, Brazil, and elsewhere; over the last few years, hundreds of thousands of people who live in what are in effect police states have mysteriously disappeared in the middle of the night without a trace; there are rumors from whistleblower politicians and scientists that these disappeared people have been transferred to those complexes to become BIVed; and so on. You can see how at least one BIV hypothesis – "I have become a BIV as the result of these mad scientists" – could become something close to a live possibility for almost any person.

My point here has nothing to do with any argument for skepticism. Instead, it's this: Our protagonist could easily end up suspending judgment on almost every one of her ordinary commonsensical beliefs. She walks and talks as if she believes she drove to the grocery store and has hands, but she can suspend judgment on those propositions and she is no longer disposed to believe them.

I once had a colleague who thought I was nuts for taking seriously violently counterintuitive philosophical theories. Philosophizing that leads us to wonder whether we really know that there are trees, or whether there are any trees to know about, or whether there are non-liar true contradictions, or whether MP isn't truth-preserving when applied to perfectly ordinary sentences, comes from deeply confused thinking. Or so a great many philosophers think. Well, they are wrong, aren't they?

References

Ballantyne, N. (2014). Knockdown Arguments. *Erkenntnis*, 79, 525–543.

Bennett, K. (2009). Composition, Colocation, and Metaontology. In D. Chalmers, D. Manley, and R. Wasserman (eds.), *Metametaphysics: New Essays on the Foundations of Ontology*. Oxford: Oxford University Press.

Blackford, R. and Broderick, D. (eds.) (2020). *Philosophy's Future: The Problem of Philosophical Progress*. Hoboken, NJ: Wiley-Blackwell.

DeRose, K. (1995). Solving the Skeptical Problem. *Philosophical Review*, 104, 1–52.

Doulas, L. and Welchance, E. (2021). Against Philosophical Proofs against Common Sense. *Analysis*, 81 (2), 207–215.

Fine, K. (2001). The Question of Realism. *The Philosophers' Imprint*, 1 (1), 1–30.

Frances, B. (2017). Extensive Philosophical Progress and Agreement. *Metaphilosophy*, 48 (1–2), 47–57.

Frances, B. (2020). Is It Rational to Reject Expert Consensus? *International Journal for the Study of Skepticism*, 10, 325–345.

Frances, B. (2021). Philosophical Proofs against Common Sense. *Analysis*, 81, 18–26.

Frances, B. (2021). Metaphysics, Bullshit, and the Analysis of Philosophical Problems. *Synthese*, 199, 11541–11554.

Frege, G. (1892/1997). On *Sinn* and *Bedeutung*. In G. Frege, *The Frege Reader*, ed. M. Beaney. Oxford: Blackwell, 1997, 151–171.

Frankfurt, H. (2005). *On Bullshit*. Princeton: Princeton University Press.

Gupta, A. (2006). *Empiricism and Experience*. Oxford: Oxford University Press.

Horgan, T. (1997). Deep Ignorance, Brute Supervenience, and the Problem of the Many. *Philosophical Issues*, 8, 229–236.

Keller, J. (2015). On Knockdown Arguments. *Erkenntnis*, 80, 1205–1215.

Kelly, T. (2008). Common Sense As Evidence: Against Revisionary Ontology and Skepticism. In P. French and H. Wettstein (eds.), *Midwest Studies in Philosophy: Truth and Its Deformities*. Hoboken, NJ: Wiley-Blackwell.

Kripke, S. (1979). A Puzzle about Belief. In A. Margalit (ed.), *Meaning and Use*. Dordrecht: D. Reidel, 239–283. (Reprinted in N. Salmon and S. Soames (eds.), *Propositions and Attitudes*. New York: Oxford University Press, 1988.)

Kyburg, H. (1961). *Probability and the Logic of Rational Belief*. Middletown, CT: Wesleyan University Press.

Ladyman, J. and Ross, D. (2007). *Every Thing Must Go: Metaphysics Naturalized*. Oxford:Oxford University Press.

Lewis, D. (1973). *Counterfactuals*. Cambridge, MA: Harvard University Press.

Lewis, D. (1983). *Philosophical Papers*, Vol. 1. New York: Oxford University Press.

Lycan, W. (2001). Moore against the New Skeptics. *Philosophical Studies*, 103, 35–53.

Lycan, W. (2019). *On Evidence in Philosophy*. Oxford:Oxford University Press.

McGee, V. (1985). A Counterexample to Modus Ponens. *Journal of Philosophy*, 82, 462–471.

McGrath, S. and Kelly, T. (2017). Are There Any Successful Philosophical Arguments? In J. Keller (ed.), *Being, Freedom, and Method: Themes from the Philosophy of Peter van Inwagen*. Oxford: Oxford University Press.

Moore, G. E. (1925). A Defence of Common Sense. In J. Muirhead (ed.), *Contemporary British Philosophy* (2nd series). London: George Allen & Unwin, 193–223.

Pedersen, N. and Wright, C. (eds.) (2013). *Truth and Pluralism: Current Debates*. Oxford: Oxford University Press.

Rysiew, P. (2021). Epistemic Contextualism. *The Stanford Encyclopedia of Philosophy*, ed. E. N. Zalta. https://plato.stanford.edu/entries/contextualism-epistemology/TS.

Schaffer, J. (2009). On What Grounds What. In D. Chalmers, D. Manley, and R. Wasserman (eds.), *Metametaphysics: New Essays on the Foundations of Ontology*. Oxford: Oxford University Press, 347–383.

Schwitzgebel, E. (2014). The Crazyist Metaphysics of Mind. *Australasian Journal of Philosophy*, 92, 665–682.

Schwitzgebel, E. (2017). 1% Skepticism. *Noûs*, 51, 271–290.

Sider, T. and Braun, D. (2007). Vague, So Untrue. *Noûs*, 41, 133–156.

van Inwagen, P. (2006). *The Problem of Evil*. New York: Oxford University Press.

van Inwagen, P. (2014). *Metaphysics* (4th ed.). Boulder, CO: Westview Press.

Weatherson, B. (2016). The Problem of the Many. *The Stanford Encyclopedia of Philosophy*, ed. E. N. Zalta. https://plato.stanford.edu/entries/problem-of-many/TS.

Williamson, T. (1994). *Vagueness*. New York: Routledge.

Williamson, T. (1997a). Imagination, Stipulation, and Vagueness. *Philosophical Issues*, 8, 215–228.

Williamson, T. (1997b). Replies to Commentators [Horgan, Gomez-Torrente, Tye]. *Philosophical Issues*, 8, 255–265.

Williamson, T. (forthcoming). Disagreement in Metaphysics. In M. Baghramian, J. A. Carter, and R. Rowland (eds.), *Routledge Handbook of the Philosophy of Disagreement*. London: Routledge.

Acknowledgments

Thanks to William Lycan, Thomas Hofweber, John Greco, Eric Schwitzgebel, David Christensen, Louis Doulas, Jonathan Matheson, two reviewers for Cambridge University Press, and the series editor Stephen Hetherington.

For Anja, the Magic Leprechaun

Cambridge Elements ≡

Epistemology

Stephen Hetherington

University of New South Wales, Sydney

Stephen Hetherington is Professor Emeritus of Philosophy at the University of New South Wales, Sydney.

He is the author of numerous books, including *Knowledge and the Gettier Problem* (Cambridge University Press, 2016) and *What Is Epistemology?* (Polity, 2019), and is the editor of several others, including *Knowledge in Contemporary Epistemology* (with Markos Valaris: Bloomsbury, 2019) and *What the Ancients Offer to Contemporary Epistemology* (with Nicholas D. Smith: Routledge, 2020). He was the Editor-in-Chief of the *Australasian Journal of Philosophy* from 2013 until 2022.

About the Series

This Elements series seeks to cover all aspects of a rapidly evolving field including emerging and evolving topics such as these: fallibilism; knowing-how; self-knowledge; knowledge of morality; knowledge and injustice; formal epistemology; knowledge and religion; scientific knowledge; collective epistemology; applied epistemology; virtue epistemology; wisdom. The series will demonstrate the liveliness and diversity of the field, pointing also to new areas of investigation.

Cambridge Elements ≡

Epistemology

Printed in the United States
by Baker & Taylor Publisher Services